Fallen Guidon

General Jo. O. Shelby

Fallen Guidon

The Saga of
Confederate General
Jo Shelby's
March to Mexico

Edwin Adams Davis

TEXAS A&M UNIVERSITY PRESS
College Station

Library of Congress Cataloging-in-Publication Data

Davis, Edwin Adams, 1904–
    Fallen guidon : the saga of Confederate General Jo Shelby's
march to Mexico / by Edwin Adams Davis.
        p.   cm.
    Originally published : Santa Fe : Stagecoach Press, 1962.
    Includes bibliographical references (p.   ).
    ISBN 0-89096-683-4 (cloth). — ISBN 0-89096-684-2 (paper)
    1. Shelby, Joseph Orville, 1830–1897. 2. Mexico—History—
European intervention, 1861–1867. 3. Americans—Mexico—
History—19th century. 4. Texas—History—Civil War, 1861–1865.
I. Title.
E467.1.S53D38   1995
972'.07—dc20   95-12207
                                                    CIP

FOR

*"R. C." (more commonly called "Rufus,"
and, by professional friends, "Huss" or
"Rembrandt")—who is responsible for
the writing of this book.*

TO THE MEMORY OF

*Private Thomas M. Davis
and Captain William M. Greever,
My grandfathers,
Soldiers of the Confederacy*

Contents

Illustrations

EXPLANATORY NOTE

A guidon was a small pennon or guiding flag borne by a cavalry unit and used to direct its movements. It was of varying colors, was usually broad at the staff end, and was rounded, pointed, or notched at the other. Its bearer, a non-commissioned officer or enlisted man, was the guide or pivot of the troop and with it gave signals for marching, wheeling, forming, aligning, and other parade or battle commands. While inferior to the standard, in the days of chivalry it was the first color the commander of horse let fly on the field.

To the old cavalryman the guidon was more than a parade or battle flag; it was the symbol of his loyalty and esprit de corps. He followed it to battle, and for it he died.

Fallen Guidon

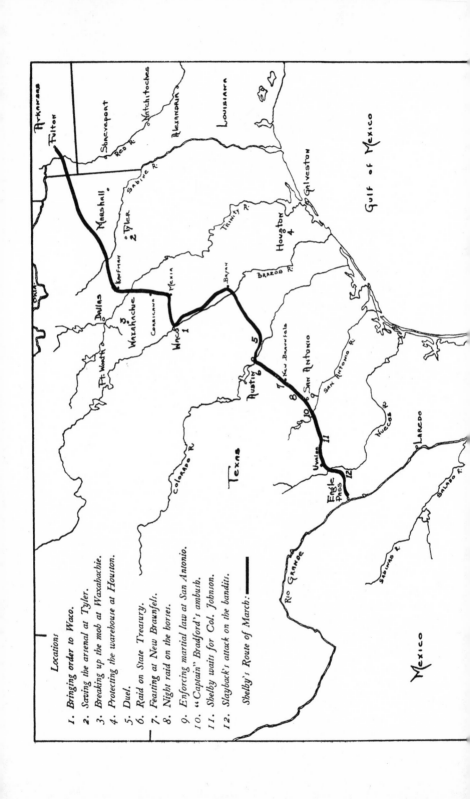

Locations

1. Bringing order to Waco.
2. Saving the arsenal at Tyler.
3. Breaking up the mob at Waxahachie.
4. Protecting the warehouse at Houston.
5. Duel.
6. Raid on State Treasury.
7. Feasting at New Braunfels.
8. Night raid on the horses.
9. Enforcing martial law at San Antonio.
10. "Captain" Bradford's ambush.
11. Shelby waits for Col. Johnson.
12. Slayback's attack on the banditi.

Shelby's Route of March: ▬▬▬

I

LAST DAYS OF
THE LOST CAUSE

1. The Road to Kaufman

THE CONFEDERATE MISSOURI CAVALRY Division
stood to horse in a column of twos at an hour before
dawn. The rested mounts were nervous and the troopers
quieted them with voices still groggy with sleep. With long-
practiced deliberation, the men cinched-up saddles, tightened
blanket straps, and hitched packs.

Ike Berry rubbed his stomach. He was a short, squat Hercules
who was free of speech and frank of nature. Ordinarily he was
slow of movement, but when aroused he moved as a tiger-cat.
In battle he always laughed, great bursts of laughter that soon
bespoke maimed and dead men. He was always hungry; only
when eating was he serious. What little reverence he had came
from the appetite. The crumbs that sometimes fell from his long,
yellow beard were at once his homage and his benediction.

Berry spoke without looking at the man behind him, "We're
two hours late this morning. It ain't like Old Jo, and it ain't
like Colonel Ben, either."

"Ben must have over-slept." Joe Moreland's tones carried
humor and comradarie, but still had sleep in them. He reached
over and patted the shoulder of his horse, a black which had
been taken from a dead Yankee after the Second Newtonia.
The low voices of the men rolled slowly around them.

Colonel Ben Elliott walked his horse, posting the line just as
he had done since joining Jo Shelby's first command as a captain, shortly after its organization in 1862 at the old red-brick
Methodist Church which stood on the bluffs overlooking the
winding Missouri at the western end of Waverly. He had been
with Shelby ever since, a fighting officer who seldom smiled, a

3

grim warrior out of the Crusades whose four battle wounds attested his headlong charges.

Then Martin Kritzer's bugle call broke through the dripping trees and the foggy pre-dawn twilight. The men mounted and put their horses at a walk. The Division moved off from the river, the battery and the baggage train lumbering heavily ahead of the rear guard, and soon picked up Trammel's Trace, the old road which led from the Red River town of Fulton in southwest Arkansas to Boston in northeast Texas and beyond.

An hour after daylight the Division crossed McKinney's Creek and three hours later passed the state boundary line and dropped off the ridges onto the rolling lands of Texas.

General Jo Shelby and his aide, Major John Edwards, had gone down to Marshall, Texas, a few days before for conferences, and the command had been ordered to Kaufman, a small village lying on the east bank of the King's Fork of Cedar Creek, a hundred and seventy-odd miles southwest of Fulton.

It would be an easy march, made without haste and without difficulty during those spring days of 1865, for there were no Federals in the area and the ferries over the Sulphur Fork of the Red River, Big Cypress River, and the Sabine would handle the battery and the wagon train. Crossing these streams presented no problems to cavalrymen who during the past three years had covered most of the heavily rivered and mountainous northern two-thirds of the Trans-Mississippi Department.

During those past three years the war in the Department had been quiet camp life and a holiday parade for some, constant, never-ending marches, raids and battles for others. Shelby's command belonged to the latter group, having been the fightingest and most ably led cavalry force west of the Mississippi, perhaps of the entire South.

It possessed a certain dashing *élan* too, an *esprit de corps* unexcelled even by Jeb Stuart's command in Virginia, and it followed an exaggerated code of chivalry unusual even in the old South. John Edwards wrote that they had fought "Yankees, Dutch, Indians, Negroes, ironclads, alligators, fever, smallpox, starvation, and wintry blasts, and never once retired from any of these without defiance on their battered crest, and ranks closed up and serried."

4

Its men were recruits rather than draftees, young men intelligent, fit, and patriotic to the cause of the Confederacy. They had come from the Missouri and North Arkansas farms of a pastoral America, had fished and hunted and loved the woods, plowed and harvested, laughed and sung at their work, played country pranks and indulged in reveries which are the parents of sadness.

They were cavalrymen of the kidney of the old German, Marshal Vorwarts of Napoleon's day, who had spent twenty years in the saddle and who, when he wished to sleep well at night, took off one spur, and who, if he wished to sleep really luxuriously, took off both.

They were supposed to wear gray uniforms, but frequently wore anything they could get, with multi-colored seams and darns and patches; they followed crude, homemade flags into battle and never admitted that their cause had been lost.

Shelby's command had been the finest raiders of all who had fought along that long, irregular front which extended from Chesapeake Bay to the bluffs of Westport Landing, near Kansas City. The raider was a new piece on the military chessboard; he must be intelligent, skilled in his trade, have a certain indifference, hardihood, a man who would have shouted with Machel at Waterloo: "The guard dies, but never surrenders." He must be "a magnificent athlete, a gladiator like Spartacus," must be able to "ride forty miles a day, fast, starve, sleep in the saddle, read by moonlight, fight eight hours in twenty-four, dazzle by speed, and electrify by the triumphs of physical endurance as well as by his genius."

The Iron Brigade, as Shelby's first outfit had been called (and the name was later applied to the Division), had known lonesome roadsides and thickets and patches of timber by night, when the weird laughter of the owl was the fabled chooser of those who on the morrow were to die for God and the Confederacy. It had known many a stormy battle day when men fell from front and flank, many a bivouac, when the twin furies of hunger and the cold of winter flew low over the sleeping camp, many a desperate raid when the wounded had no succor and the dead no sepulchre. It had been consecrated to brotherhood and the Cause by the constant presence of fatigue and

5

Cavalry charge at Battle of Pea Ridge, 1862.

death, fatigue which brought fanciful dreamings to the soldier's mind and complete insensibility to bodily pain, death which had come swiftly in battle or slowly and softly in delirium from the bleeding wound or the disease-wracked body.

Its marches and raids and battles have been all but forgotten—marches that covered over a hundred miles in less than twenty hours; raids like the Great Raid into Missouri in 1863, when it moved to the Missouri River and back again, fifteen hundred miles in thirty-four days, fought a dozen battles in an area filled with 50,000 enemy troops, killing, wounding or capturing over 1,100 Federals, and capturing or destroying over $2,000,000 worth of supplies and property.

6

A wild charge saved the day at Marshall, Missouri, where 1,200 men were surrounded by more than 8,000 better equipped and supplied soldiers of the Union. Novelist Paul Wellman, while still a writer for the Kansas City *Star,* wrote vividly of that charge: "The Union volleys rolled up a typhoon of sound. The first horsemen in the charging force went down but the leader's black plume still floated. The raiders plunged squarely into the gray powder cloud ahead of the fire. There was a shock, the rapid tattoo of revolvers, and the glitter of sabres. Then the Confederates were through—miraculously, unbelievably through. How they did it will always remain a mystery but they actually sheared through Ewing's line as if it had been made of cheese instead of men and found themselves free on the other side."

The Battle of Westport has been forgotten, the greatest battle fought west of the Mississippi, the "Gettysburg of the West," and the second Battle of Newtonia, the last important engagement of the Civil War fought in the Trans-Mississippi Department, after which Confederate General Sterling Price admitted that Shelby was the best cavalry officer he had ever seen.

But the soldiers of the Iron Brigade had also known days of carefree camp life. There had been days when food was plentiful, when whole oxen had been roasted and hams boiled over open fires, when corn fields had been stripped of their roasting ears or gardens plundered of fresh turnips and onions, or when sorghum, fresh from the small horse-driven, mountain mills, had been lavishly poured over oven-baked bread made of wheat flour.

There had been those two months spent at Camp Nannie Wilson, on the south side of White River near Batesville, eighty miles northeast of Little Rock, Arkansas, where cavalry drills became tournaments of medieval knights and sham battles were fought with all the trappings of chivalry, and where there was laughter at the antics of Postlethwaite, artillery Major Dick Collins' black bear cub who had ridden a gun carriage into battle and who now feasted on sweetmeats and was petted by rough and soft hands.

A silken Confederate flag had been presented to the Brigade, a banner which was to wave over many a long march and

7

desperate battle and which was to find its final resting place, the last flag of a defeated Confederacy, beneath the muddy waters of the Rio Grande.

At the end of that winter of 1862-63, the men rode out with their hats decorated with blood-red sumac leaves.

The war went on, and in September, 1864, Shelby and his men accompanied Price's Raid into Missouri, according to Edwards, the "stupidest, wildest, wantonest, wickedest march ever made by a general who had a voice like a lion and a spring like a guinea pig." The Brigade fought, and most of it rear guard action—after Westport, hundreds dead; after Mine Creek, a command torn, bleeding, decimated; the Second Newtonia, a battle "stern, unforgiving, bloody beyond all comparison for the stakes at issue," a battle where the Brigade's fighting surpassed any that Union General James Blunt had ever seen.

The retreat southward from Newtonia was a hideous nightmare. Flour gave out, then meal and meat and medicines. Recruits gave up in spirit but the battle-scarred veterans cheered them on. Three days south of the Arkansas River hunger found an ally in smallpox. Battles were a challenge to a man's body and his soul; fever could not be fought. But the Brigade's organization held, the thing that had become a tradition, a grim war spirit, a thing of guarded Gray glory.

After that the Trans-Mississippi Department went to sleep. Fifty thousand soldiers sat on their arms. General Kirby Smith, like Stonewall Jackson, believed in prayer, but while Jackson trusted in his prayers *and* his battalions Smith trusted only his prayers. No move was made to aid a doomed South; shortly it would be guillotined.

The Brigade (at this time it was officially the Missouri Cavalry Division) was finally ordered to Fulton, Arkansas, to report to General James F. Fagan, who was organizing an expedition against Little Rock. Days were passed in the activities of preparation—cleaning and repair of equipment, constant training, camp guards, picket guards, advanced posts. The men were ready, confident, but the movement against Arkansas's capital never materialized.

Then the news of Lee's surrender broke like a tidal wave over the Trans-Mississippi Department. First came unbelief, then fleeting resolutions of courage and defiance, then a reaction of timidity and despair of some officers and men.

Filled with all the agony of the Confederate position, Shelby assembled his command, "felt its tired heart . . . told them calmly the dark tidings, and issued an address to his soldiers which exhorted them to heroism, faith, hope, and endurance."

"The crisis of a nation's fate is upon you . . . I conjure you to stand shoulder to shoulder and bide the tempest out . . . I promise to remain with you until the end. To share your dangers, your trials, your exile, your destiny, and your lot shall be my lot, and your fate shall be my fate, and come what may, poverty, misery, exile, degradation . . . Meet at your company quarters, look the matter fairly and squarely in the face . . . Stand together, act together, keep your discipline and your integrity, and all will be well, as you strike for God and humanity . . . If Johnston follow Lee, and Beauregard and Maury and Forrest all go; if the Cis-Mississippi Department surrender its arms and quit the contest, let us never surrender. For four long years we have taught each other to forget that word, and it is too late to learn it now . . . *This Missouri Division surrender*—My God! Soldiers, it is more terrible than death . . . We will stand together, we will keep our organization, our arms, our discipline, our hatred of oppression, until one universal shout goes up from an admiring eye, that this Missouri Cavalry Division preferred exile to submission—death to dishonor."

The men cheered him to the echo and held their organization and their discipline.

Shelby sent Colonel John Thrailkill and Major R. J. Lawrence to Shreveport, Louisiana, headquarters of the Department, for orders, ammunition, and additional artillery.

A few days later he and Major John Edwards went to Marshall, Texas, in order that he might be nearer departmental headquarters, obtain a better view of the rapidly passing events and, at the same time, to be not too far distant from his command, which was moving from Fulton across northeast Texas to Kaufman.

So the Iron Brigade rode out from Fulton, crossed Red River and moved southwesterly along Trammel's Trace, leisurely and without haste.

2. Indecision, Chaos, Surrender

AS JO SHELBY and his adjutant rode across the spring-awakened countryside to Marshall he should have realized that with the surrender of Lee at Appomattox the Confederate States of America had been dealt a mortal blow from which there would be no recovery. With that surrender the defending lion of the Confederacy, borne backward in his leap at Gettysburg, had died. The Old Imperial South had been beaten to its knees—to a man upon his knees every attacking enemy is a giant.

Lincoln had been the war's great strategist, its guiding military genius. Lincoln's military greatness was real; that of Jefferson Davis imagined. And from a far richer North he had provided the men and materiel. Grant had only to grunt and the earth shook with the tread of marching, well-equipped reinforcements, to nod and new batteries wheeled into line, to wave his hand and troops of fresh cavalry galloped past. At the rate of six to one Grant had ground Lee to powder, not through battlefield genius but through sheer power, a heavyweight taking the futile blows of a bantamweight and waiting to deliver the one knock-out punch.

For the next two generations the South would try to explain how the war might have been won. If Albert Sidney Johnston had not died at Shiloh, if Stonewall Jackson had been spared the bullet of his own men at Chancellorsville, if Davis had let Lee have his head. But history does not live by hindsight explanations.

As the Confederacy was organized it could never have saved itself, whatever might have been its industrial and manpower potential, for politicians moved in with the yell of States' Rights almost before it had put its armor on. Strict constructionists of the Confederate Constitution sang and fiddled and danced while Rome was burning. Armies pled for arms and ammunition, food, clothing and medicine while clerks and even cabinet officials quarreled among themselves, indexed reports and pointed out that requisitions would have to go through regular channels.

But after the death rattle of the Confederacy had begun the Trans-Mississippi Department finally stirred itself to punitive action, action which could better have been taken during the sum-

"Last review in the Confederacy."

mer of 1863 when Vicksburg and the entire Mississippi Valley had been lost.

On April 21, 1865, General Kirby Smith prepared a stirring appeal to the soldiers of his department and three days later it was read to the troops on dress parade at Shreveport: "The crisis of our revolution is at hand. Great disasters have overtaken us. The army of Northern Virginia, and our Commander-in-chief are prisoners of war. With you rest the hopes of our nation, and upon your action depends the fate of our people." But a Federal spy reported that the appeal had little effect upon the troops, that the men were dejected, and that mutiny and wholesale desertion were openly discussed. The Department rapidly crumbled, a department of 60,000 troops, many of whom had never fought a battle nor fired a shot at the enemy.

General Simon Bolivar Buckner begged Governor Henry Watkins Allen of Louisiana to come to the old French Louisiana town of Natchitoches to address the demoralized and disbanding soldiers. Allen went, met a division near Mansfield and,

11

nearly weeping, pathetically pled with them. The men crowded around him and promised to stand firm, but after he had departed forgot their promises.

He returned to Shreveport and called a public meeting on April 29 for the purpose of considering "the wants and conditions of the country, and of suggesting such measures as may be necessary to encourage our people and promote the success of our Glorious cause." Thousands came and the exercises continued from eleven in the morning until after four in the afternoon. Kirby Smith was there, and Buckner and Sterling Price, Governor Thomas C. Reynolds of Missouri, and Judge W. B. Ochiltree of Texas.

But the soldiers were apathetic; one of them wrote: "Mass Meeting today. Thayee and I listened awhile. Sun was hot, audience cold and speeches as far as we heard good in their way . . . Allen's remarks abounded in poetic imagery." It was late in the day for poetic imagery.

On May 8 Colonel John T. Sprague of the United States Army arrived at Shreveport and promised Kirby Smith the same surrender terms which Lee had accepted, but Smith rejected the proposal—an army not immediately threatened could not "afford to surrender as prisoners of war."

Governor Allen then called a conference of the Trans-Mississippi governors to meet at Marshall, Texas. Smith at last was roused, believing that his department still held firm; with his "strong, fresh and well equipped" army the capital of the Confederacy might be transferred west of the Mississippi.

To the Marshall meeting came Allen of Louisiana, Reynolds of Missouri, and Harris Flanagan of Arkansas, while Pendleton Murrah of Texas, who was dying of tuberculosis, sent Guy Bryan as his representative. It was decided that Allen be appointed to visit the Federal authorities to discuss the complete pacification of the Department, but Colonel Sprague refused to let Allen accompany him through the Federal lines—"I did not feel at liberty to give a safeguard to the governor of a rebel State."

A few days later Allen wrote to his friend Sarah A. Dorsey that he would stay at his post as long as he was needed and then find asylum "as an exile in a strange land . . . within the next sixty days I shall in all probability be on my way to Mexico."

The civil authority of the Department had capitulated; what would the military do?

Most of the important army officers had also come to Marshall: Smith, Buckner, Shelby, Preston, Walker, Fagan, Parsons, Churchill, Hawthorne—all except "Prince John" Magruder. Perhaps Magruder heard a rumor of what Shelby was about to do; perhaps he was jealous of the fiery leader of the Iron Brigade.

Buckner called a night conference after the governors' meeting. All were present except Smith, who knew they were about to depose him.

Shelby addressed them: "The army has no confidence in General Smith . . . We should concentrate upon the Brazos River. We must fight more and make fewer speeches . . . fifty thousand men with arms in their hands have overthrown, ere now, a dynasty and established a kingdom. Every step to the Rio Grande must be fought over, and when the last blow has been struck that can be struck, we will march into Mexico and re-instate Juarez or espouse Maximilian. General Preston should go at once to Marshal Bazaine, and learn from him whether it is peace or war. *Surrender is a word neither myself nor my division understand.*"

Shelby infected them with his enthusiasm. His words took root. His hearers began to envision and to dream—a splendidly armed and equipped army, with silver spurs, scarfs, plumes, and flags, and all the accouterments and pomp of war, an elite force like the black mousquetaires of Louis XIII who, clad in all the coquetry of lace and frills and scented gloves, had stood saucily by and with laughter watched the linesmen falter at the breach, then without a break in step had swept through it, leaving two-thirds of their number dying or dead upon the ground. A vast new empire would be born to which Southerners who did not choose to live under a Yankee yoke could repair and build anew their proud and chivalric South.

"Who will lead us?"

Shelby and Reynolds had already talked to Governor Allen— they would give him supreme command—but he had refused to leave his civil duties, and his friends were teasing him by

13

calling him "the Emperor," appointing themselves to imaginary posts of honor and giving themselves imaginary and fanciful titles in the imaginary and fanciful imperial court.

"Who else but Buckner," replied Shelby. "He has rank, reputation, the confidence of the army, ambition, is a soldier of fortune, and will take his chances like the rest of us."

A worse choice could not have been made. It had fallen to Buckner's lot to surrender Fort Donelson, after the escape of Generals Floyd and Pillow. His later record as a Confederate field officer had not been brilliant, as a commanding general mediocre. He was an impractical businessman who was given to writing verse. He was certainly no soldier of fortune. Nevertheless, in the absence of "Prince John" Magruder, he was the ranking officer next to Smith, had a splendid physique (women had called him the hero with a form like a war-god) and was wearing a brand new uniform glittering with gold lace and silver stars. He was elected by the cheering group and made a short speech of acceptance in which he promised never to entertain thoughts of surrender.

But Shelby was still in command of the conference. He urged that General Smith immediately be informed, that haste was needed: "I shall march tomorrow to the nearest enemy and attack him. Have no fear. If I do not overthrow him I will keep him long enough at bay to give time for the movement southward."

The meeting adjourned and Shelby called on Kirby Smith. Few words passed between them.

"The army has lost confidence in you, General Smith."

"I know it."

"They do not wish to surrender."

"Nor do I. What would the army have?"

"Your withdrawal as its direct commander, the appointment of General Buckner as its chief, its concentration upon the Brazos River, and war to the knife, General Smith."

"What do you advise, General Shelby?"

"Instant acquiescence."

Shelby's coup had succeeded. He had cast a spell upon the older and more conservative generals and they had complied with his wishes.

14

The plans were agreed upon. Shelby was to march to Shreveport and commence operations against the nearest Federal forces. Kirby Smith was to move his headquarters to Houston, leaving Buckner in command at Shreveport to begin the consolidation of the armies of the Department west of the Brazos.

But the very moment Shelby galloped away, the generals settled into abject apathy, and urged Buckner to surrender. What now of his promises, his newly received authority? What now of his brilliant new uniform and his brightly burnished sword in its brightly burnished scabbard? He had surrendered the first army of the Confederacy; was he now to surrender the last?

Buckner's enthusiasm died. There was a romantic element in his nature, yes, but it was overweighed by indecisiveness. His heart had never really been fired. And Preston already on his way to Mexico.

Shelby learned of Buckner's indecision. Only two courses of action were left. He could throw his command on Shreveport, seize control of the government, and appeal to the army to carry out the original plan of defending the line of the Brazos River, or he could attack the Federal forces wherever found and make surrender of the Trans-Mississippi Department impossible.

John Edwards drew up a proclamation for his commander and it was printed on wall paper, the only newsprint available: "Soldiers, you have been betrayed. The generals whom you trusted have refused to lead you . . . Lift up the flag that has been cast down dis-honored. Unsheath the sword that it may remain unsullied and victorious. If you desire it, I will lead; if you demand it, I will follow. We are the army and the cause. To talk of surrender is to be a traitor. Let us seize the traitors and attack the enemy. Forward, for the South and Liberty!"

So Shelby and his men rode out from their camp at Stone Point, near Kaufman, and were soon on the march toward Corsicana, where they would turn eastward to Shreveport. But the rains came; rains that were an inundation. Bridges were swept away, roads became quagmires, water rose to the saddle girths. They finally forced their way through to Corsicana.

During those last days the wildest rumors had been flying throughout western Louisiana and Texas. Smith would fight

15

on . . . Buckner was now the commanding general and Buckner would fight . . . Jefferson Davis had arrived in Shreveport.

But in reality the armies had begun to disintegrate, for officers had lost all power to control their men. At Alexandria, Louisiana, Assistant Adjutant General David F. Boyd wrote to Colonel Amedee Bringier of the 7th Louisiana Cavalry: "All is confusion and demoralization here, nothing like order or discipline remains . . . There are but eighty-six men at the forts . . . in a word, colonel, the army is destroyed and we must look the matter square in the face and shape our actions (personally and officially) accordingly."

Lack-luster Louisiana soldier Edwin H. Fay wrote to his wife: " 'Tis useless to disguise the fact that Gen'l Lee has sold the Confederacy." In Texas, where were the "three-foot" Bowie-knives and the coiled lassoes which would be used if the invader came? Where were the warriors who had cried that if the Yankees dared "to pollute the sacred soil of Texas, every rivulet should run with blood and every bayou should be a battlefield"?

Not being able, due to the cutting of telegraph lines and the breakup of the courier system, to communicate with Kirby Smith, Buckner called a meeting of the generals in Shreveport. Surrender was agreed upon. Officers were sent to Baton Rouge for a preliminary conference with General Francis Herron of the Federal Army, and on May 26 at New Orleans Buckner surrendered all the Confederate forces west of the Mississippi River, subject to the approval of Kirby Smith. The articles of agreement were dispatched by special steamer to Galveston.

On May 30 Kirby Smith wrote to Colonel Sprague that he was a general without an army. "The army in Texas disbanded before my arrival here . . . The Department is now open to occupation by your Government."

Anarchy reigned in western Louisiana and Texas. The soldiers had not been paid for months and as their armies broke up they found immense stores of supplies. The pillage of warehouses, treasury offices, manufactories, and quartermaster and commissary trains began. Clothing, food, horses, mules, wagons, tents, guns and ammunition—everything that was transferable was plundered.

Kirby Smith's disbanded army returns home.

The mania for plunder rapidly seized civilians, and men and women gathered in bands in towns and villages, broke into warehouses and helped themselves to cloth, sugar, coffee, and luxuries which they had long been denied, luxuries which had been hoarded by leeches who had been sucking at the life blood of the Confederacy.

Governor Allen of Louisiana and Governor Murrah of Texas did what they could, went about their duties with calmness and self-control. Should they go into exile? Should they remain at their posts and wait for the occupying Federal troops? Then news came of the arrest of governors east of the Mississippi. Their friends counseled them to escape to Mexico. Finally word

17

came of the surrender of the Department and that Kirby Smith would soon affix his name to the official documents.

On June 2, Allen addressed his last message to the people of Louisiana: "My administration as Governor of Louisiana closes this day. The war is over, the contest is ended . . . Now let us show to the world that as we have fought like men— like men we can make peace . . . I invite the closest scrutiny, not only of these papers, but to all my acts as Governor of Louisiana . . . I go into exile not as did the ancient Roman, to lead back foreign armies against my native land—but rather to avoid persecution, and the crown of martyrdom . . . If possible forget the past. Look forward to the future. Act with candor and discretion, and you will live to bless him who in parting gives you this last advice."

On the same day General Kirby Smith went on board the United States steamer *Fort Jackson,* lying off Galveston harbor, and signed the articles of surrender. The American Civil War had officially ended. Confederates began wearily to walk or ride into United States army encampments to secure paroles.

But stationed at Corsicana, Texas, was a command which still kept its discipline and its organization. Its camp routine— guards and pickets and advanced posts, formation movements and sabre drills and pistol practice—continued as if the Confederate surrenders had been but phantom rumors floating over the South.

One day a dozen new recruits mutinied and whined to be permitted to go home. Shelby's patience broke. He tied them into pairs and sent them under guard to the nearest Federal post, as men who had mistaken the command and had enlisted in the wrong army.

Then a courier arrived from Kirby Smith with the order for Shelby to march to Shreveport and surrender his command to General John Pope. The men flew into a rage, charged Smith with deeds he had never done, pilloried him for permitting his army to melt away, for allowing his department to have become a barrack-yard of Yankee regiments, and "his military star went down behind a cloud, and the drama closed upon a bent and irresolute pilot . . . whose hands were so delicate and soft from inaction that when the storm came fiercely and vast, they could neither reef the dangerous sails nor put the trusty helm hard up before the wind."

What were the alternatives? Shelby and his men could continue fighting for the cause that was now definitely lost until they were overwhelmed, they could disband and go home, or they could march as a unit into exile, to a promised land in Mexico.

That night the men talked of those alternatives, and Jo Shelby, their leader on a hundred hard-fought fields, wrestled in his Gethsemane.

3. The Missouri Cavalry Division's Last Night

THE USUAL noise and raillery of camp was missing that night. The men performed their duties with few words and then sat around the fires talking in low tones. They considered what decision they would make on the morrow. Old Jo would not again lead them to fight for the South. That was certain, for they all knew that nothing could be gained by fighting. The war had ended.

Most of them probably put off the decision for they were thinking of the past, of comrades dead, of hardships and suffering, of half-forgotten incidents of camp life. . . .

The day Major David Shanks had fallen heavily to the ground, the Federal giant who had shot him lying mortally wounded not four rods away. And Shelby coming up . . . the tears from eyes unused to weeping . . . the short goodby and Shelby riding swiftly away, not daring to look back at the spot where he had left his reckless fighting and generous comrade. . . .

The day the champions had fought in front of the armies just as they had done in the age of chivalry when knights wore greaves and vizors and when the battle-cry was "St. James for England." Colonel Alonzo Slayback, a royalist who believed in kings and queens, rode to the front, faced the Union cavalry, and issued a challenge to single combat. A renegade Arkansan named Wilhite galloped to within twenty paces and fired at Slayback. Two shots later Wilhite had a bullet in his thigh and had retired. Two other duels followed and the Confederate did

19

not receive a scratch. Cheers rang out along the line, hats were doffed; then the Rebel yell, and the wild charge. . . .

The ambush which had been set on the road between Cassville, Missouri, and Fayetteville, Arkansas, along the overhanging ledge of rocks (a deadly spot for I have seen the place). Colonel David Hunter's men waiting in eager suspense . . . The Federal detachment riding merrily along in a column of fours. The signal and the merciless fusillade and eighty men lying on the ground dead and a hundred more wounded, while riderless horses rushed frantically from beneath the deadly rocks. . . .

The day that Arthur McCoy—the dashing devil-may-care St. Louisan who had won honors at Shiloh, who always rode to the front before a charge, doffed his plumed hat to the adversary, and murmured "*en garde*" through his moustache—had ridden silently upon a score of Union Indians sleeping alongside a rail fence and had sabered seven of them with his own hand. . . .

The night the "tall, lank, kill-dee sort of fellow," a bushwhacker, had darted furtively into camp, thinking they were Yankees, and had bragged of his murders and his plunderings of Southern sympathizers, saying proudly, "They were Rebels, you know." And Shelby, slowly growing set of face, turning to Ben Elliott: "Take this man to the rear and shoot him." Then the fear in the man's eyes and the sagging of his legs as he was dragged away before he could speak. . . .

But all of it was not bloody and wretched and hideous.

Remember that night just out of Lewisville, Arkansas, when Joe Thomas and James Moreland had brought the barrel of whiskey into camp. Each had a wonderful knowledge of sacred and profane history and so for an hour they had debated that if a wooden Trojan horse had contained armed men, might not a wooden whiskey barrel contain whiskey—while the men laughed and pled and threatened. . . .

Remember the Battle of the Beehives? The log cabin on the hill surrounded by shrubbery and trees? No one noticed the beehives. The charge up the slope and the enemy's twelve-pounder howitzer sending its fourth shell (maybe it was the third) right into the line of hives, splintering or knocking them over. Then the cloud of buzzing, stinging insects, creating havoc among the horses, the battle-line giving way, the men riding this way and that to avoid the bees, Shelby swearing and storming at them until he himself was attacked, then riding into the clump of bushes in a vain attempt to lose them, while his men roared with laughter and yelled taunts at him. . . .

Remember the night Dick Gentry, with a well-filled and bleeding sack slung across the pummel of his saddle, boldly rode his horse into the creek where Old Jo was watering his mount? And Old Jo questioning him? And Dick saying that he was coming down to wash his clothes. And Old Jo remarking, "You'd better get back to camp or your clothes will bleed to death." Then Gentry lodged in the guardhouse. And afterward the quarter of fresh pork being mysteriously found by Old Jo's tent, and Shelby ordering Dick released, saying laconically, "No use keeping a man shut up all his life for a little laundry."

These incidents and a hundred more welling across the years.

Some of the men looked over at Shelby, who was gesturing and talking with Major John Edwards, the Adjutant.

Their leader had been a young Kentucky cavalier who had migrated to Missouri in 1852. Connected with some of the most noted families in the Blue Grass region, he had disappointed many of the belles of Lexington when he had departed for what they considered a wild frontier.

He had settled at Waverly, which lay on the south bank of the Missouri River about three hundred miles west of St. Louis. During the fifties it was a town of growing importance, boasting a flour mill, a ropewalk, a foundry, a blacksmith shop, several warehouses and general stores, and a number of sturdy, frame houses. In partnership with his stepbrother, Howard Gratz, he farmed 500 acres of land, managed a ropewalk and a sawmill, and soon established a commission and general merchandising firm.

In 1858, at the age of twenty-seven, Shelby married Elizabeth Shelby, the seventeen-year-old daughter of his father's first cousin, and with a large party of friends embarked for a river steamboat honeymoon to St. Louis. Two years later came the fateful election and the Civil War had begun. His men well knew what he had done since that time.

He was still a young man in his early thirties who, although

21

recently commissioned a Major General, still wore the buff sash and wreathed stars of a Brigadier. Alongside him on the ground was a black felt hat, its front brim turned up cavalry style, its golden band holding the long black plume which had been added after the First Newtonia and which had become as famous west of the Mississippi as Stuart's was in Virginia. His uniform . . . well, he didn't pay much attention to uniforms when he was in the field. Like Stonewall, anything would do.

His face was square and massive, topped with chestnut colored hair (though after the war some of his men recalled that it was brown and others that it was coal black and still others that it was golden, "like the sun") and hanging from his chin was a luxuriant growth of beard with mustachios, which he sometimes curled after the fashion of Napoleon the Little. One of his Arkansas sergeants recalled that "he was the finest looking man I ever saw, black hair and handsome features." His build? It was that of a cavalryman, straight and tough and sinewy.

There were other things: the electrical quality that carried men with him, which drove them without being driven; the shrewd intelligence of things military; a certain infectious, indomitable will; and that something which called forth loyalty and pride and *esprit de corps.* You can have your Stonewalls and your Forrests and your Albert Sidney Johnstons and that Louisiana Frenchman who loves his full name, Pierre Gustave Toutant Beauregard, even Marse Robert himself. We'll take Old Jo.

But he had an uncontrollable, savage temper at times, which revealed him not uniform but obliquely cut. He had many facets, and as Federal Judge John F. Philips, an old Union veteran, said, when he gave the funeral oration over Shelby's body years later: "There were no dead planes, no monotonous levels in his journey through life, and it ran along rugged mountains, cataracts and varying scenery, much of it exciting, and much of it beautiful."

His face was sometimes hard and pitiless, but the anger was soon softened and melted away by irrepressible, genial smiles. Warring natures and extremes met within his disposition—he was all dignity and discipline or all laughter and hilarity; "lenient

22

today, the men sported with his mood; tomorrow his orders were harsh as sullen drums. In the languor of camp life he might be listless and contemplative, or nervous, energetic and rapacious for air and exercise as a Comanche brave." He would discuss politics and war and crops with his men or with farmers who crowded his quarters; then the mood would change and he would wave his hand and gallop off to join his troops who were drilling and maneuvering.

Yes, there were peculiar facets to this man. He was as good as any man in the Confederate army with profanity, yet he never swore when his aide, a Methodist preacher named Mobley, was within hearing distance. He superstitiously favored beginning his cavalry movements at midnight, much to the grumbling of the men. He had a constant fear of losing his artillery, though Dick Collins, throughout the entire war, never had a gun captured. And he would ride only sorrel horses—during Marmaduke's stubborn retreat at Cane Hill (when Shelby was covering the rear) he had four sorrels shot from under him and afterwards would never ride another animal but of that color.

Some of the men argued that when in battle he was impervious to pain. At the Battle of Helena a Minie ball had entered his right arm at the elbow and had gone down its entire length and out at the wrist. And Major Jacob Stonestreet, who was standing by him at the time, always maintained that "he did not even draw in his breath." But the arm had bothered him for months and the fingers had so stiffened that for the rest of his life he could barely manage to fire a revolver or to write his name and never again could grip and swing a cavalry sabre.

He was born to be a tough, rugged leader of soldiers. After the old first company had been enlisted he had made a short speech (his speeches were not orations for he was not a polished orator) in which he said that he wanted no man who was not willing to enlist for the duration of the war.

That he was brave there was no question. The Kansas historian, William E. Connelley, called him "one of the bravest and truest soldiers that ever shouldered a musket in America."

He had military genius and, as his adjutant later wrote, "an almost infallible divination of the enemy's designs." General Alfred Pleasanton, of the Union cavalry, said that he "was the

23

best cavalry general of the South. Under other conditions he would have been one of the best in the world."

Shelby believed as Marmont, one of Napoleon's Marshals, had believed, that "the chief of an army must provide for the well-being of the soldier, and know, on important occasions, how to partake of his sufferings and privations." And he had always carried a large sum of clean United States bills with him for supply money, for he realized that many Confederates, particularly late in the war, did not trust the money of the Confederacy, and his men must be supplied.

But he drove his men as he drove himself, for to him "an army ever should be a machine, perfect in all its parts—dumb, soulless, brainless, with power only to be moved, to throb and to pant, to crush and to grind at the bidding of one supreme engineer, who knows when to apply the steam and to set in motion all its thousand springs and axles of gigantic strength."

His men thought of these things as they watched their commander sitting with his adjutant by the fire.

So much for Shelby; what of Shelby's men? Who were these men who had followed him since he had organized his first company, or had come later to the outfit, and who had lived through the bitter, bloody years, to this last day, when Armageddon had been lost.

For the most part they were Missouri farmers and small-town tradesmen, with a sprinkling of Arkansans. Most of them were young, though a few had the gray hair of age. They were tough and lean. They were . . . Let time roll back the years. . . .

There, sitting at the fire with Shelby and Edwards, are George Hall, the boy orderly, Shanks and Hooper and Gordon, and a few others smoking, talking, planning for the morrow. Over yonder is Sears, the scout, with his long fair hair and his kindly face. There is Yandell Blackwell humming snatches of battle songs (though his favorite song was "Villikins and His Dinah") and puffing lazily on a captured meerschaum. There sit Jim Wood and Charley Jones and Newton Hart arguing the relative merits of beef over mutton. Over there is Captain Williams polishing his brace of revolvers. And there are Neale and Toney reading love letters and "laughing in amorous glee as some soft, melodious sentence came stealing up."

24

There is June Terry, the Brigade surgeon, a veritable gallant who according to rumor, had once swum two bayous and broken his horse's leg in a rickety bridge to get a piece of blue ribbon and a tangled, perfumed lock of hair.

There is Crispen, one of the finest cavaliers of them all, with a keen zest for a sonnet and the archest smile for a woman. There is Major Lawrence counting his greenbacks to see if there are a sufficient number to purchase a jug of apple-brandy. There is Crittenden reversing the old axiom and contending that "to the victor belongs *not* the spoils." There is Arthur McCoy telling how he went smugly into St. Louis and drove out a wagon loaded with seven hundred thousand musket-caps. Peter Trone is over there preaching an imaginary sermon to a group who appreciate his inimitable acting. Dan Ingram and Pat Marshall are filing notches in their pistol-butts for Yankees killed.

And there is old, romantic Maury Boswell—"Uncle Morry"— a three hundred pound giant who had made every exhausting march and ridden in every headlong charge. He had done everything and had done it just a mite better than the next man— helped build roads where roads were impossible to build, grown corn where none would grow, been an apothecary, a doctor, a farrier, a carpenter, a horse-trader, a surgeon, a farmer, a lawyer, a preacher, a magistrate, and, in the Old War with Mexico, a fabulous artillerist, and, to top it all, had been a Methodist and a Catholic at the same time.

Shelby still sat by his fire, planning for the future, and John Edwards, the Chevalier Bayard of Missouri, sat with him, penning his words, putting onto paper chivalrous, romantic expressions which he had never said, but which he would have uttered had he had the knack.

Shelby recalled reports coming out of Washington. The Mexican Legation, where Matias Romero represented the Juarez Government, was filled with men volunteering for service in Mexico. General Grant was sympathetic to the idea. Sherman and some of the other generals were interested, and Schofield was willing to lead the army that would push the Emperor Maximilian and Marshall Bazaine, who commanded the French legions that supported him, into the sea at Vera Cruz. But Seward believed that diplomatic pressure would be sufficient.

Juarez accepted his plan, though he would have preferred a few of Sherman's regiments.

In addition to these reports, Shelby had received a letter from his cousin, General Francis Preston Blair, Jr. Blair had written that President Lincoln was of the opinion that the war would soon be over and he would be glad for ex-Confederates to cross the Rio Grande into Mexico, join Juarez, and defeat the combined forces of Maximilian and Bazaine. Then they could "look around them to see what they could see, occupy and possess lands, keep their eyes steadfastly upon the future and understand from the beginning that the future would have to take care of itself."

Shelby had received no official communication on this matter, but he could trust his cousin. Here was a way in which ex-Confederates could save their honor, and at the same time gain new lands and riches in that land south of the Rio Grande.

To Shelby the plan was practical. Thousands would come to him from all parts of the Confederacy. Some of his own men—this must be accepted—would wish to return home. But as for the rest—they had never heard his voice but to obey. The Brigade still held its organization and its discipline. The Banner of the Bars still waved from its headquarters.

The War between the States had been a woman, winning as Cleopatra, with crowns and garlands and caresses for sturdy service. But the long and bloody jousting for her favors had been lost. There was today to think of, and tomorrow. Put the bitter past where it belonged, a Dead Sea behind them—a strange, new land and an empire awaited but to be taken, an empire south of the Rio Grande.

II

THE MARCH BEGINS

4. The Missouri Cavalry Division is Dead; Long Live the New Iron Brigade!

THE CAMP FIRES BURNED low and went out; only the tiny flares of the picket fires broke through the black darkness of the Texas night. The men dreamed. Some dreamed of home and families. Some dreamed of Mexico and the riches of Guanajuato, Taxco or the hills back of Pachuca. Others heard in the darkness the clanking of steel scabbards, the cries and oaths of the men, the neighing of horses, and the steady, rhythmic tramp, tramp of the march, as of waves breaking on a beach or the continuous, low rumble of thunder at sea. Some saw Death riding through the night, as it had done a thousand times in the past, to ready itself for the bloody work at daylight and enfold young and stalwart fellows who were lusty food for gunpowder and fit to cross the chasmal gulf of that yonder to claim all the odalisques and houris which would be their reward in a warrior's paradise.

The sun was shining, the floods had subsided, and the prairie grasses were blankets of waving, undulating green, when Shelby's Missouri Cavalry Division rose from its last bivouac. It was the last organized military unit of the Confederacy still holding the Stars and Bars proudly to the wind.

Three days before, Kirby Smith had written a postscript to a letter addressed to Colonel Sprague of the United States Army: "Since writing the above, I have information that the Missouri and a portion of the Arkansas troops still retain their organization." Now the Arkansans had disbanded.

The usual camp routine was followed that morning—horses watered, fed, and rubbed down, bedrolls shaken out and aired, breakfast cooked. It was another morning of a thousand such camp mornings. There was no haste. There were jokes and un-

27

accustomed silences. The morning details completed, the men lounged around, waiting for assembly. Martin Kritzer would sound his bugle when Old Jo was ready.

Major John Edwards, the Adjutant, worked in his tent, appearing now and then to talk with Shelby, who sat silently and foreboding.

A native Virginian, Edwards had come to Missouri as a youth of fifteen or sixteen and had settled in Lexington to learn the printing trade at the office of the *Expositor*. He had joined Shelby when the first company had been organized at Waverly and, despite his youth (he was only twenty-four at the time), had moved up to the rank of Major within little over a year. He soon became Shelby's Adjutant and remained in this position the rest of the war.

He was not a physically robust man, but was wiry, nervous and tense, quick and pointed in his movements. At times he was introspective and at such times was hard to live with. His face was round and childlike, his forehead high, his eyes luminous, liquid, and dark blue, innocent in that they constantly beheld a world of romantic wonders. He had the poise of a fine head and a noble bearing, but a drooping mustache at times gave his mien a solemn, tragic cast.

He had an impulsive, poetic temperament, was mild-mannered, courteous and kind (he tore up his shirts for wounded men and gave away his horses), was sympathetic and at times shy, but his face would fire with fury during battle and then relax in dreamy repose during moments when there was no fighting to be done. Long after the war his old commander said that "he was the bravest man in war and the gentlest man in peace I ever saw."

With him the war had been a great crusade, for he lived in a world of romantic, illusive imagery, a world of battlements and turrets, waving banners and horsemen in armor, where the sun illumined the castles and reflected itself back from the burnished shields and gleaming blades. His writings were filled with references to and quotations from the romantic writers.

To John Edwards, Shelby's men were Douglasses, Rolands, Coeur de Lions, Bruces—all the great host of chivalry—and he had so fired them with his own romanticism that a hundred

28

little evidences of chivalry became a part of their lives as members of a fabulous cavalry troop. And he had spurred them on to heroic exertions; after all, had he not had more horses shot from under him than any man in the Brigade?

His official battle reports and military communications, signed of course with Shelby's name, were written in this florid vein and many modern historians, not knowing, have given Shelby credit for them:

"Long before the full round moon had died in the lap of the dawn; long before the watching stars had grown dim with age."

"It was a beautiful moonlit night. White fleecy clouds hovered over the sleeping river, over the doomed craft with all her gala lights in bloom, and over the crouching lines of infantry and the yawning cannon . . . Just as the white hand of morning put away the sable clouds of night four pieces of artillery sent their terrible messengers crashing through the boat."

"Driving the frightened Federals before them like chaff before the winds of heaven,

    Tramp, tramp, along the land they ride,
      Splash, splash, along the lea;
    The scourage is red, the spur drops blood,
      The flashing pebbles flee!"

Flamboyant, overly dramatic, out of time and place—here was an accoutered knight charging with lance at rest against rifled cannon. But it was the way Edwards lived; it was the way he wrote.

So Major John Edwards worked in his tent, drafting Shelby's last appeal to his men, planning as a grand marshal the last formation.

The summer sun climbed the sky. Then came Martin Kritzer's bugle call. The men of the Missouri Cavalry Division stood to horse, mounted, and passed in last formal review before the old banner of the Division.

History does not record Shelby's last speech to his men. Edwards, in his memoirs, does not record that he made a speech at all. But Thomas Westlake, who scribbled his notes without the aid of a dictionary on a trio of scratch pads, stated that "in the morning General Shelby formed his men around him on the open Pearie and made a Speach to them Recounting many

29

of the hardships and Struggels of the four years past. He said he was not going to surrender but was going to Mexico and Requested all that would to go with him."

Perhaps Shelby spoke the words that Edwards may have written. If so, he painted pictures of the past in bold and vivid colors, recounted hardships and victories—how he and his men had fought a hundred battles, had ridden on many an intrepid raid, had fought and died together. But the war had ended; they were the only Confederates still under arms. Why try to evade the bitter truth. The choice was now surrender or flight. But flight need not be unplanned, futile, useless, or cowardly. Yonder to the south lay the Rio Grande and beyond it Mexico, where a foreign prince, Maximilian of Austria, who had established a puppet kingdom of France, sat upon a gilt and tinsel throne and was even now fighting to the death for his empire against the poor and scattered Liberal forces of Benito Juarez, the Indian of Guelatao.

Was ever a better opportunity offered to men of courage and spirit? Beyond the Rio Grande lay an empire which could be had for the taking. And Southerners would go there with the blessing of the American government. Once this news was broadcast, fifty thousand men would spring from the scattered forces of the old Confederacy.

If they chose to fight for the Emperor his throne would be secured; if they supported Juarez and the Liberal cause the Mexican Republic would rise again. In either case they would be the deciding force, would rise to a position of dominance in the new regime and would establish a sort of new Confederate States of America in the land beyond the Bravo.

The call ran down the ranks for volunteers to Mexico. Several hundred men rode to the front.

The last goodbyes were said. Those who chose to return to their homes and families dispatched a delegation to General Buckner to inform him that they had elected not to go to Mexico, "that they had fought for the Confederacy, were still ready to fight for it, as long as a man remained, but if the country was to be given up, they intended to surrender like soldiers." These men gathered their belongings and started for Marshall or Shreveport to secure paroles.

The Missouri Cavalry Division and the old Iron Brigade were dead; long live the New Iron Brigade!

Those who had elected to go with Shelby immediately proceeded to the organization of the new brigade. Shelby was nominated for colonel and elected with a shout, receiving every vote but his own, but "some who had been majors came down to corporals, and more who had been lieutenants went up to majors," and each demotion was received with raucous laughter and each promotion with wild cheers and Rebel yells.

Playfully calling his old veterans young recruits, Shelby called his new officers together and ordered the old routine of drills to begin, for Texas must be crossed, an unorganized, lawless, bloody Texas, then Mexico, with its fighting Juaristas or veteran battalions of Bazaine. Then he and Edwards began to plan the route of march, the equipment and supplies to be taken, the minutia of military detail.

There was work to be done before they left Texas, for some order must be brought out of the chaos. In middle May, Governor Murrah had written: "In some sections, society is almost disorganized; the voice of the law is hushed, and its authority seldom asserted . . . Murder, robbery, theft, outrages of every kind against property, against human life, against everything sacred to a civilized people, are frequent and general . . . The rule of the mob, the bandit, or unbridled passions, rides over the solemn ordinances of the government. Foul crime is committed, and the criminal, steeped in guilt, and branded by his own dark deeds with eternal infamy, goes unwhipped of justice."

Equipping the expedition was not difficult for Texas was filled with newly-imported or abandoned military supplies. To Shelby's battery of rifled cannon was added ten new Napoleon howitzers, together with 600 rounds of ammunition. Within a few days 6,000 new British Enfield rifles, just landed and with the Queen's arms still upon them, were secured, along with 40,000 rounds of small arms ammunition and bushels of gun caps and pistol cartridges. Five hundred heavy dragoon sabres were distributed.

Every man was equipped with an Enfield rifle, a Sharpe's carbine and four heavy-calibre revolvers, with a hundred and twenty rounds of ammunition for each, a sabre, and a brace of

Bowie knives. The new Brigade was an arsenal; what it lacked in numbers it made up in fire power and fighting equipment.

For a week the Brigade remained at its camp near Corsicana making preparations for the march across Texas and Mexico and enjoying luxuries to which the men were unaccustomed, for they had appropriated the goods of a newly-arrived wagon train—dried fruit, bacon, pickles, preserves, whisky, molasses and other delicacies. There was little discipline after the day's drills, but the drills were just as they had always been—long and sweaty, with oaths, and tired beasts and men.

At last the preparations were completed and Shelby called a council of his officers, who sat around a circle, Indian fashion— Williams, Collins, Langhorne, Blackwell, Elliott, Gordon, Slayback, Jackman, and a few others.

"Before we march southward," said Shelby, "I thought we might try the range of our new Napoleons."

There was no reply, but the men looked at each other with sly smiles as they divined his intentions.

"There is a great gathering of Federals at Shreveport, and a good blow in that direction might clear up the military horizon amazingly."

Still no reply. They knew what was coming.

"We might find hands, too, we might find hands for our six thousand bright new Enfields. What do you say?" There was a wistfulness and a pleading in his voice. He was still a Confederate soldier, hoping to battle the enemy.

They argued the proposal but decided against it. Their faces had been pointed toward Mexico; to Mexico they would go.

5. Bringing Order to Central Texas

THE NEXT morning the Brigade stood to horse, mounted and at the old cavalry command of "Forward, Ho," moved off toward Waco. At the rear followed the battery and the wagon train, loaded with supplies and luxuries enough to carry the outfit all the way to Eagle Pass on the Rio Grande.

Confidence rode the ranks and Shelby could say as Napoleon had once said, "The company is the unit. It is my captains who have won all my victories. Drill for me your companies perfectly

32

and I will do all the balance." The movement, precision, and bearing of the individual soldier had never been better, even in the most glorious days of the Old Iron Brigade.

The expedition moved slowly and without haste, taking two days to traverse the thirty miles to Mexia. At old Fort Parker, a few miles south of Mexia, the Brigade turned westward to Waco.

Waco was filled with disbanded and lawless soldiers. Shelby put the place under martial law, mobilized a group of citizens into a vigilance committee, helped old Bayliss Earle rebuild his cotton mill, the machinery for which he had run through the blockade during the war, and furnished a convoy to the Mexican firm of Gonzales and Company so it could send needed goods southward to less favored communities.

From Waco, Shelby turned southward toward Bryan, following the valley of the Brazos. This was plantation country and before the war had been as rich as any in the South; now there was desolation, livestock gone, fields unplanted, ex-slaves straggling without food or shelter about the land.

As he moved southward from Waco, Shelby heard that the arsenal and gun manufactory at Tyler was threatened by a roving band of bushwhackers, so he dispatched Colonel Yandell Blackwell with a small troop to break up the band and restore order. Within hours Blackwell was in Tyler.

The troop took position in front of the building and that night several hundred of the bushwhackers gathered there and demanded surrender.

Blackwell strode forward. "We have yet to understand that word. These are Jo Shelby's soldiers, and therefore you are mistaken. Pray teach it to us."

The mob insisted. If he would not surrender at least he could give them the guns and ammunition.

"You can't have any," said Blackwell.

"We will take them."

At this Jim Franklin, Tom Cordell, Clay Evans, Dan Franklin, Jim Ward, Tom Collins, and a few others sauntered up to Blackwell's side.

Blackwell again addressed them: "You have been soldiers, and you wish to deter soldiers of your own cause from doing their

33

duty. It is a long time since we tasted blood, and you are welcome to Tyler and all its contents, if a man among you dare to march five paces forward to an attack."

Not a sulker moved, though from the rear the shrill voices of their women urged on the cowards.

Then Jim Kirtley, Sam Downing, Albert Jeffries and Jim Rudd seized kegs of powder and advanced beyond Blackwell, leaving behind them a dark and ominous train of powder. Placing their kegs in a semi-circle about the entrance to the arsenal, they connected the keg holes with the train of powder. The mob surged back.

"What do you mean?" they yelled.

"To blow you into hell," Kirtley sang back at them, "If you're within range while we are eating our supper . . . we are hungry. Good night."

Blackwell's men went back to the business of preparing supper. The mob began to disperse. By daylight the town had been cleared. A few days later Blackwell and his troop rejoined Shelby.

Waxahachie sent a supplication for help, for it was being tyrannized by a mob of Union and Confederate deserters. Shelby hurried off fifty men under Maurice Langhorne, who rode through the town like a whirlwind and swept it bare of bullies in a single night.

Leaving half a dozen men under Lieutenant Cochran to guard the town, Langhorne rode off to rescue a wagon train of flour.

The ominous groups which soon began to gather about the street corners indicated to Cochran that trouble was at hand. His resolution was taken in a moment. Calling three of his men, he instructed them to ride separately a mile from town, then join and gallop back with furious noise and clatter. This was done. A large crowd immediately gathered around the dusty couriers, one of whom handed Cochran a portentous dispatch which read to the effect that Shelby's advance was within a mile of the town and that it would camp there for the night. In the face of possible reinforcements to the small garrison, the mob dispersed.

But after Langhorne returned the mob again formed and marched on the Confederate depot. Backed by his men, which

34

Railroad depot in Houston, from an old print.

included such veterans as Bud Pitcher, Jim Crow Childs, and John and Martin Kritzer, Langhorne faced them.

Before the war Langhorne had been a Methodist preacher but after the beginning of the fighting had joined Shelby and had become one of the best of his men, and one of the best pistol shots in the Brigade. He was a quiet man, who seldom swore, and had a voice gentle as a school girl's.

"Go away," said Langhorne, mildly, his voice soft as a minister's at prayer, his face stern as an avenging angel.

The mob fired a volley and Langhorne's men rode forward in wild attack. Sabres rose and fell and revolvers cracked, while the plunging horses rode down the mob. It was a Second Newtonia, a Marshall, a Westport, and a hundred other furious fights all rolled neatly into one little fray and over in a few moments.

When morning came the mob had evacuated the town, leaving their dead and wounded behind. Langhorne soon rejoined the Brigade with additional stores of flour and other needed supplies.

Upon reaching Bryan, Shelby heard that trouble was brewing in Houston. Not once invaded or even seriously threatened, Houston had never heard the roar of hostile cannon and its citizens had received the news of Lee's surrender with ears that

35

did not quite believe the truth. One woman remarked that she would fly to the islands of the sea and "live there in everlasting solitude" before she would "live the subject of a conqueror." A Confederate officer noted that he had heard some "bad reports" from east of the Mississippi, "but I don't believe the people there are whipped, and if they are, we are not, and can not be whipped here."

But the war had ended and chaos reigned in Houston. Rapacious ex-Confederates were soon joined by lawless elements from all the Trans-Mississippi West. These hoodlums paraded the streets, frequented the numerous and "really magnificent" saloons for which the town had become noted, and then spilled out into the streets in a weaving, staggering search for ramshackle brothels along the back alleys, or luxurious rooms and apartments of higher-class ladies of easy virtue in the town's best hotels. Houston was a Sodom and a Gomorrah set on the muddy banks of sluggish Buffalo Bayou.

Three weeks before, a mounted detachment of ex-Confederates from Debray's Brigade had broken ranks and had joined a mob which looted the ordnance and clothing depots, yelling that they were distributing among themselves the possessions of the late Confederacy. After this lawless work had been done, soldiers from Galveston had arrived and, finding the booty· gone, had angrily threatened to pillage the town. These elements still milled about Houston, gambling, drinking, fighting, killing without provocation, so an appeal was sent to Shelby.

Shelby called for captains James Meadow and James Wood. "Take one hundred men and march quickly to Houston. Gallop oftener than you trot. Proclaim to the Confederate women that on a certain day you will distribute to them whatever of cloth, flour, bacon, medicines, clothing or other supplies they may need or that are in store."

The two officers nodded.

"Hold the town until that day, and then obey my orders to the letter."

"But if we are attacked?"

"Don't wait for that. Attack first."

"And fire ball cartridges?"

"And fire nothing else. Bullets first, speeches afterward."

36

The troop moved south to Houston and found a clamorous mob besieging a warehouse near the railroad depot.

Wood and Meadow drew up in front of the throng.

"Disperse!" they ordered.

The mob opened up and its leader strode forward. "After we have seen what's inside this building, and taken what's best for us to take," he said, "we will disperse."

The troop of horse sat waiting.

"The war's over, young fellows, and the strongest party takes the plunder. Do you understand our logic?"

"Perfectly," replied Wood, "and it's bad logic if you were a Confederate, good logic if you are a thief. Let *me* talk a little. We are Missourians, we are leaving Texas, we have no homes, but we have our orders and our honor."

Perhaps Wood squared his shoulders a little more firmly then.

"Not so much as one percussion cap shall you take from this house until you bring a written order from Jo Shelby, and one of Shelby's men along with you to prove that you did not forge that order. Do you understand *my* logic?"

And as the scene was described years later: "They understood him well, and they understood better the one hundred stern soldiers, drawn up ten paces to the rear, with eyes to the front and revolvers drawn." Shrill voices from outside the mob howled it on, urged the thieves to fire, but not a shot came.

Then they began to drift away, singly or in small groups. Within a few minutes the mob had dispersed and before the evening had passed "the streets of Houston were as quiet and as peaceful as the cattle upon the prairies."

A few days later, their mission accomplished, Wood and Meadow rejoined the Brigade.

Shelby, meantime, had moved southwestward along the old Spanish *Camino Real,* or King's Road, which had been built during the Spanish colonial period from San Antonio northeastward to Nacogdoches, San Augustine, and the settlements in eastern Texas and western Louisiana. It missed Austin, the capital, by only a few miles. Shelby turned northwestward at the Colorado River toward Austin.

But before Austin was reached a tragedy occurred, one of those sudden and bloody incidents which were a mistaken part of the code of chivalry which the South had long ago appropriated.

The custom of dueling had been brought to the American colonies within a few years after the Virginia Colony was settled but it had never taken firm root in the North. After the American Revolution, however, the South generally adopted the practice and codified rules and regulations. In settled or urban areas it was practiced with strict conformance to the New Orleans or Charleston Code, but in more remote rural sections it frequently reverted to bloody forays akin to old frontier gouging matches. During the Ante Bellum era it reached into all levels of Southern life and, although Confederate government and state officials had tried to outlaw it during the war years, it had persisted—particularly in the army.

Two officers of the Brigade—a captain and a lieutenant—quarreled over the affections of one of the light-of-love women camp followers. She was the captain's by right of discovery and prior possession, but one night she deserted him for the favors of the lieutenant. The argument between the two men was heated and the captain ended it by slapping the lieutenant full in the face.

"You have done a serious thing," said one of his comrades.

"It will be more serious in the morning," was the quiet reply.

"But you are in the wrong and you should apologize."

The captain only tapped the handle of his revolver. "This must finish what the blow has commenced. A woman worth kissing is worth fighting for."

The challenge was given and the terms agreed upon by the seconds—a revolver and a sabre, from horseback, twenty paces apart back to back, at the signal wheel and fire, advancing or remaining stationary as each man chose.

Though dozens of the men knew of the coming affray, Shelby was not told. It was well known that he had never permitted dueling in his command. He had always arrested the would-be principals and forced a compromise, just as he had done a few days previously when a quarrel had led to a challenge.

Early the next morning the men stole away from camp singly or in small groups. Arriving at the appointed ground, they arranged themselves in two long lanes, some distance apart. There was little talking as the principals rode up, took their places and received instructions.

Both men were calm. On the captain's face was a half-smile. His body already bore the scars of a trio of battle wounds. What had he to fear from this almost beardless boy.

The men sat lightly in their saddles, each poised for the wheel and charge.

"Ready—wheel!"

The trained battle-mounts whirled as if on pivots.

"Fire!"

The captain's horse sprang forward; that of the lieutenant never moved.

The captain rode down upon his adversary, firing as he came. Three chambers were emptied, but to no effect.

Now he was almost abreast of the lieutenant, who still had not fired. The charging horseman leveled his revolver again, but before he could fire the lieutenant raised his revolver and sent a bullet through the captain's brain. He was dead before he hit the ground.

They buried him just as the sun arose, then rode silently back to camp. Shelby immediately called a parade mount, lectured them, raged at their disobedience, issued a general order for the execution of the surviving participant in any future duel and placed the entire command under strict discipline. Then, chastened, with parade stiffness in the saddle, the Brigade turned toward Austin.

6. Austin

IT WAS late on a cloudless afternoon when Shelby and his men rode through heat waves that shimmered over the dusty wagon road, down gentle slopes covered with cedar and live oak, mountain laurel, redbud and huisache, catclaw, Indian blanket and sumac, and into the capital city of Texas.

Austin was a shabby little town with tree-lined, dusty streets, squalid collections of rude huts and cabins and false-fronted, ramshackle stores, a few larger, even elegant houses, and government buildings, which lay up Congress Avenue about a mile north of the Colorado River. The ten-year-old, native-stone state capitol was flanked on the northwest by the Supreme Court building, which during the war housed a cartridge and percussion cap factory, and on the southeast by the State Land Office. To the southwest, across the street, was the governor's mansion, a rather stately and classic structure built in the Greek Revival style, with tall Ionic columns backed by the typical Southern gallery. A few blocks southeast was St. David's Episcopal Church, while in the opposite direction rested the old and empty home of ex-governor E. M. Pease. Over on Robertson Hill in East Austin was the former French Legation, designed and built by Count de Saligny, Chargé d'Affaires to the Republic of Texas from France, and at the time of its construction during the early 1840's the most pretentious building in Texas.

The Brigade passed through the south section of the town, forded the Colorado, and went into camp at Barton Springs, near the old grist mill, in a narrow little valley lying between two hills with grassy slopes and limestone ledges covered with laurel, sycamore, elm and twisted live oak trees, and through which ran a tumbling, gushing creek.

The men went about their camp duties with cheerful alacrity for they had been in the saddle for some days and had dreamed of a night or two in what Texans called the "metropolitan" capital. Here—such was the Texas conception—society was "elevated," with charming and beautiful women to illuminate it, and pleasant walks and elegantly-appointed saloons. It was an attractive prospect for cavalrymen who had had little time for relaxation since the beginning of the war.

Mess over, the men left camp in small groups and wandered into town, and along streets filled with crowds of paroled soldiers, refugees, inevitable ruffians, women and playing children, Negroes selling all manner of objects—buttons and pins, tape, pen staffs, powder and shot and caps, fruits and vegetables, and cooked dishes from their sidewalk stands. The crowd was loud and assertive and the loungers milled about.

Clouds gathered as night came on, then mist, and finally rain, great gusts of it blown by a gathering wind. The women and children disappeared, but groups of men continued to roam aimlessly along the streets.

The state capitol at Austin housed the state treasury as well

State capitol at Austin, Texas, in 1865.

as a sub-treasury department of the Confederate government. In the building's five safes were over three hundred thousand dollars in gold and silver, guarded by only a few soldiers.

This treasure tempted the notorious guerrillas of a certain "Captain" Rabb, a half *ranchero,* half freebooter-bushwhacker who for months had terrorized the area. Taking advantage of Shelby's arrival in Austin, he planned a raid on the State and Confederate treasury, hoping that the blame would fall upon Shelby and his men.

Early on the rain filled night Rabb's raiders filtered into town and, as the night progressed, took their stations unnoticed in dark places awaiting the signal to attack. At the appointed signal they converged and rode hard for the capitol. They swept aside the few guards, shot them down, rushed into the building, and began to hammer at the iron doors of the safes. The alarm was sounded and church bells began to ring. The home guard company mustered at the armory. The Mayor sent a messenger posthaste to Shelby.

41

Then from across the Colorado came the full, resonant blare of Martin Kritzer's bugle sounding the rallying call. In a few moments a cavalry column, four deep, headed by Jim Ward, galloped into the square.

"They are battering down the Treasury doors," said the Mayor.

"I should think so," replied Ward. "Iron and steel must soon give way before such blows. What would you have?"

"The safety of the treasure."

"Forward, men!" yelled Ward and the detachment rode off at a trot through the gate of the capitol grounds.

Lights shown from the windows of the building through the rain and inside the raiders could be seen milling about. The few guards stationed outside fired an ineffective volley and disappeared into the state house, which Shelby's men quickly surrounded. Not a command had been given—this was ordinary work for men of the old Iron Brigade.

Then Rabb's men rushed out, their arms filled with plunder. There was a sudden, pitiless flash of flame from two score Sharpe's carbines, and following it the cries of wounded and dying men. The survivors ran back into the shelter.

Ward yelled the charge and his men swept through the doors. From inside there came the sound of shots and cries and of men falling on the echoing wooden floors—then the lights went out and there was stillness, and through the gloom and smoke and shivered glass and scattered gold and silver they dragged the raiders—bleeding, dying and dead.

Then a great-framed giant appeared. In his drunken greed he had taken off his pants and had tied the legs tightly at the bottoms. An epicure, his pants and hat were filled with gold pieces, for he had not deigned to touch the silver. He staggered out toward Ward's posted guards, refused the command to halt and fell, shot through by three bullets fired from a distance of only two or three paces.

Rabb, with several of his men, had escaped at the beginning of the attack and had carried with them a blanket filled with some fifteen thousand dollars in gold and silver. In their haste, however, one of the corners became untied and for a mile the streets along which they fled were scattered with the shining coins.

42

The massacre over, guards patrolled the blood-stained state house and its grounds. The crowds which had gathered melted into the night. The remaining hours of darkness quietly passed.

In Austin Shelby met Captain A. B. Miller of the Confederate supply department. Miller was one of the most remarkable men of the Confederacy. Under his administration guns, cannon, ammunition, clothing, hats, shoes, and other supplies had poured into Texas and western Louisiana, for his wagon trains were constantly on the road between Matamoras, Mexico, and Shreveport.

Captain Miller and Governor Murrah urged Shelby to take the Confederate treasure and use it to pay his own unpaid soldiers and others with whom he might come in contact. Murrah argued that Shelby's command was the last organized body of Confederate troops in Texas. But Shelby replied that although they still carried their Confederate flag the war was over and that they were on their way to Mexico to seek their fortunes with either Benito Juarez or the Emperor Maximilian.

The temptation was strong and the arguments telling, but Shelby and his officers never wavered. Shelby knew what would be said if they appropriated the gold and silver and he and his officers would never be subject to malicious condemnation.

"I went into the war with clean hands," said Shelby, "and by God's blessing, I will go out of the war with clean hands."

During those days since the surrender of the Department his line of march had been so straight as no longer to leave his destination a matter of doubt. Confederate fugitives had sought shelter under his flag and within the ranks of his veterans. He, like the rest of his men, was penniless and homeless, but the possessions of the Confederate States of America, in all right, should return to the authority of the state in which they were located; they should not be given to individuals, be they soldiers or civilians. The future was uncertain for him and his men and he might have argued, as had ex-Senator Trusten Polk of Missouri, "These fellows will carry me through, but they will find for me no gold and silver mines."

From Austin, to New Braunfels, to San Antonio, to Eagle Pass, Shelby would not impress anything for his men or his horses, not even a sheaf of oats. He foraged upon the prairies,

43

paid for all the supplies with captured United States currency, treated citizens with courtesy, and carefully repressed anything that savored of lawlessness. He was determined to leave Texas and the Confederacy without a stain upon himself and his men. That he succeeded is a matter of history.

From Austin Shelby moved toward San Antonio. He passed through San Marcos, which nestled at the crossing of the San Marcos River, a village surrounded by springs and steep, wooded hills, and went on to New Braunfels.

New Braunfels was a neat German village with a faintly Old World atmosphere. It had been established back in the 1840's by that quixotic Prince Carl Zu Solms-Braunfels, who arrived with a large retinue of velvet-clad courtiers and soldiers wearing cocked hats bedecked with brilliant plumes. He built his fort on a hill overlooking the surrounding countryside where he lived in the style befitting a prince of the blood. He returned to Germany after the annexation of Texas and his settlement had grown and become prosperous.

The people of New Braunfels gave Shelby and his men a hero's welcome and there was feasting while lager beer ran clear and cool.

Leaving New Braunfels, the Brigade moved across short-grass, mesquite-covered prairies or low hills toward San Antonio. It was a lawless land where trouble might be encountered, and Shelby ordered all the old rigid practices of war carried out—scouts and camp guards, pickets and advanced posts.

One night forage was scarce in the immediate vicinity of the camp site and the horses were posted under guard at a grassy place some two miles distant. Night scouts were ordered out, for the animals were magnificent and in good condition—a great temptation for the ruffians and border thieves who filled Texas.

The camp had hardly settled down for the night when Martin Kritzer, who in addition to his bugling doubled as a scout, rode up. He was typical of the Old Brigade, an intelligent and tireless cavalryman who could go for long periods without sleep.

"Well, Martin," said Shelby.

"They are after the horses."

Shelby called to Captain Maurice Langhorne, who appeared, as he usually did, with a quiet smile etched on his face.

"Take fifty men and station them a good half mile in front of the pasture."

Langhorne nodded.

"There must be no bullets dropping in among our stock, and they must have plenty of grass room. Station the men, I say, and then station yourself at the head of them. You will hear a noise in the night—late in the night—and presently a dark body of horsemen will march up, fair to see between the grass and the sky line. You need not halt them."

Langhorne knew what was coming.

"When the range gets good, fire and charge."

Langhorne selected his fifty troopers and rode off at a gallop. Within an hour he had stationed his men. They waited, silent and alert, on the ground, holding the reins of their mounts. The hours passed. Then they heard the low sounds of advancing horsemen and with the skill born of long war years estimated their numbers.

"Get ready. They are coming."

The men slowly pulled themselves from the ground and slipped into their saddles, bending low over the necks of their horses.

A dark mass slowly rose over the horizon and Langhorne asked, "Are you all loaded?"

And someone replied, "Have been for four years."

The advancing mass separated into distinct shapes, the stars gleaming down on their polished gun barrels.

"They have guns," said Langhorne, "but no scouts in front. What would Old Jo say to that?"

John Kritzer laughed. "He would dismount them and send them to the infantry."

"Make ready!" The old Methodist preacher gentleness had returned to Langhorne's voice. His men slowly brought up their carbines and rested them over the necks of their horses.

"Take aim!" It was a low command, really not a command at all so softly was it given. Langhorne, the preacher, was about to give the benediction.

"Fire!" This time it was a shout, a Rebel yell welling over the prairie that carried a chilling terror in it.

The rifles cracked as one shot, the flaming patches of fire

breaking through the night. Yells broke out and cries, while horses upreared and bolted and men reeled and fell from the saddle. Then Langhorne's men swept forward in a wild, headlong charge.

As Edwards later described the scene: "A red cleft in the heart of the midnight—a murky shroud of dun and dark that smelt of sulphur—a sudden uprearing of staggering steeds and staggering riders—a wild, pitiful panic of spectres who had encountered the unknown—and fifty terrible men dashed down to the charge. Why follow the deadly work under the sky and the stars. It was providence fulfilling a vow—fate restoring the equilibrium of justice—justice vindicating the supremacy of its immortal logic."

And Edwards continued: "Those who came to rob had been a scourge more dreaded than the pestilence—more insatiate than a famine. Defying alike civil and martial law, they had preyed alternately upon the people and the soldiers. They were desperadoes and marauders of the worst type, feared and hated or both. Beyond a few scattering shots, fired by the boldest of them in retreat, they made no fight."

The next morning when the Brigade moved off toward San Antonio, it passed thirty-nine unburied bodies lying on the ground face downward in grotesque positions, or face upward and gazing with sightless eyes at the rising Texas sun.

III

ACROSS SOUTH TEXAS TO THE RIO GRANDE

7. San Antonio

SHELBY'S COMMAND GALLOPED INTO San Antonio about daybreak on the morning of June 16, two weeks after General Kirby Smith had signed the articles of surrender of the Trans-Mississippi Department—the last formal surrender of organized Confederate forces.

San Antonio, like Houston, had been one of the few boom towns of the Confederate South, for it was the immediate gateway to Mexico and the contraband trade, and to it had flocked lawless, unscrupulous, fortune-hunters of both North and South. From an isolated little island in the almost boundless land that was southern Texas, the old half-Mexican, half-American town, which had lived through the bitter days of the Texas Revolution, the capture of the Alamo and the massacre of its defenders, had emerged into a boisterous youngster with a population of ten thousand people.

San Antonio had witnessed exciting events during the early days of the war. Here General David E. Twiggs had surrendered the Department of Texas to Major Ben McCulloch's Confederate forces. Lieutenant Colonel Robert E. Lee had passed through from Fort Mason, which lay at the northern edge of the hill country overlooking the Llano River, where he had been stationed, under orders to report in Washington, D. C. Mc-Culloch had urged Lee to join the Confederacy at that time, but he had refused. Lee had finally been permitted to depart, but without his baggage, which he never recovered. John Baylor had recruited his Partisan Rangers in San Antonio in 1862. By 1863 the town had furnished forty companies to the Confederacy and had become a lusty, roistering border boom town.

Some weeks before Shelby's arrival, Captain A. B. Miller

had sent him an urgent request for two squadrons of cavalry, in order that he might seize the Confederate sub-treasury at San Antonio and appropriate its gold to pay the soldiers who had straggled into the town. But Shelby had refused anything that gave the appearance of violence.

A horde of hungry Texans, "wild as prairie wolves and as relentless as Cossacks," had soon after captured the treasury, and had destroyed, stolen or scattered all of the goods that packed the Confederate warehouses. The majority had never fired a shot at a Yankee and "had never seen a Federal except in their dreams."

The worst of them had left San Antonio with their gold and goods before Shelby's arrival, but some two or three hundred still remained. San Antonio was "breathing fitfully and hard as a fevered sleeper." To the lawless elements, as well as to hungry and war-weary ex-soldiers, it was a paradise, for King Cotton, magnificent to the last, had chosen the town as his last royal seat. As one observer described the desperadoes: "These last had taken immediate possession of the city, and were rioting in the old royal fashion, sitting in the laps of courtesans and drinking wines fresh through the blockade from France."

Shelby and his command were still twenty miles from San Antonio when these rioters tried to "smoke out" merchant Tom Hindman. They pounded on his door one night and demanded entrance.

"What do you want?" asked Hindman, a small man with the courage of an old Highlander.

The leader of the attacking party replied, "It is said that you have dealt in cotton, that you have gold, that you are leaving the country. We have come for the gold—that is all."

"Indeed!" Hindman's unusually soft voice was strangely harsh and guttural. "Then, since you have come for the gold, suppose you take the gold." He did not speak another word, but no man in the mob advanced to take possession of his treasure.

A group of citizens, having heard that a raid on Hindman was planned, hurried off a messenger to Shelby at his camp on the New Braunfels road. Shelby roused his men and rode through the night to the relief of Hindman and his mob-threatened neighbors.

Shelby immediately put the town under martial law and appointed Colonel D. A. Williams provost on one side of the San Antonio River and Colonel Alonzo Slayback on the other. What one missed, the other caught, and some villains who were pressed fell into the river. As Edwards wrote, "Some men are born to be shot, some to be hung, and some to be drowned." Peace soon returned to San Antonio and of evenings men and women again paraded through the tiny squares and plazas, the old Mexican Plaza de las Armas (Military Plaza), the gardens of the Alamo, and along the streets buying hot Texas-Mexican border dishes, sweetmeats, and souvenirs at such Mexican shops as "The Dancer," "The Bad Woman," or "The Mule."

Shelby established his headquarters at the Menger House (called affectionately by some by the nickname of "Mingo's"), which fronted the Alamo Plaza at the end of Blum Street. His sentinels stood at their stations before it or paraded from post to post with military precision. His patrols sauntered along the streets quieting would-be trouble makers with a glance or a slight movement of the right hand toward the hip. Here at "Mingo's" Shelby would rest a little, while his men caught their breath and made preparations for the long march to the Rio Grande.

At the time of Shelby's arrival many of the former military and civil leaders of the Confederacy were hiding in San Antonio, for they believed that the whole power of the United States government was concentrated upon their capture, imprisonment and trial for treason.

Governor Henry Watkins Allen of Louisiana—bluff, quick and decided, idealistic and cultured and sincere, earnest, terribly in earnest—had left Shreveport and had journeyed overland with five companions, including his two servants. The day of Allen's departure from Shreveport, a close friend, Sarah A. Dorsey, had helped him pack a few necessary belongings. When she noticed that he was going to take only crude tin cups, she had given him a silver goblet which had belonged to her mother. "Keep this," she had said, "for your own personal use. It will bring back old associations—Natchez, Lake St. Joseph—all your friends to you, whenever you take a drink of water." He took the goblet and used it until his death in the City of Mexico.

49

After arriving in San Antonio Allen had written a friend: "If you are intimate with the Federal commander, give him my compliments, and say to him, that I have to ask of him but 'one favor'—that he will rule our poor people mildly, and not let them feel the horrors of subjugation. If he will do this, all my feelings of hatred and antipathy will cease, and *I will never again raise* my hand against the United States authorities, *I ask nothing* for myself. I am perfectly willing to remain in exile the rest of my life."

A friend who met him a few days later wrote home: "I met Allen on his way out to Mexico; he held out his open hands to me, saying, 'Judge, they are clean.' "

Judge John Perkins, Jr., a close friend of Governor Allen, and a member of Louisiana's Secession Convention and a representative in the Confederate Congress, was in San Antonio. Perkins had been one of the wealthiest men in Louisiana, had possessed everything that could instruct or gratify the cultural tastes of a plantation aristocrat. During Grant's advance on Vicksburg, so the story was told, he had spent one night at "Somerset," his plantation estate, "brooding amid all the luxury and magnificence of his home. He arose the next morning a stoic. With a torch in his hand he fired everything that would burn, leaving nowhere one stone upon another to tell of what had once been the habitation of elegance and refinement."

Governor Thomas C. Reynolds of Missouri—calm and self-possessed, polished, "wary as Talleyrand, stubborn as Massena"—was in San Antonio, as were generals and officers of lesser grade. Commodore Matthew Fontaine Maury of Virginia, the noted hydrographer and pioneer in oceanography, had stopped off on his way to Mexico.

"Prince John" Magruder, one of the most fabulous of the Confederate generals, who had been an officer in the "Old Army" and who had served in the Mexican War, was there. A giant of a man (he stood six feet, four inches), he looked the part of a prince or a duke, wore his uniforms with a flair, loved display and parades, and could fight all day and then dance all that night. He had a certain elegant nonchalance, too, as when he was asked at the Newport dinner party what the salary of an officer was; he had turned to his butler and had straight-

Military plaza in San Antonio, from old print.

facedly asked: "James, what *is* my salary?" Patriotism was his passion and the South was his mistress. As Edwards described him: "Tall as Wallenstein, straight as Tecumseh, . . . he could fight, dance, speak, write, plead as a lawyer and command as a despot."

These men had come to San Antonio to plan their escape from a defeated South and from the clutches of a vengeful North. Menger's Hotel became their meeting place, where they talked of old war days, checked the routes to the City of Mexico, and schemed for the future.

To San Antonio also came men looking for business, agricultural or ranching opportunities—men who hoped to get a fresh start in the frontier areas of Texas. Most of these newcomers had in pocket less than fifty dollars in United States currency, though a few, like the Greever brothers (Lieutenant Bennett Greever of Company A, 27th Arkansas Infantry, and Captain William A. Greever of Colonel Harrell's Battalion, General Cabell's Brigade), had salvaged a small amount of capital

51

from the Confederate ruins and would soon go into the freighting business.

Here at "Mingo's" past cares and troubles fell away; Shelby's men relaxed, enjoyed the offerings of the bar, joked and played pranks. Turning to song, they called for Lieutenant Jake Connor, the minstrel whom Edwards called "the inimitable Irish delineator, the chief of all serenading parties," whose rendition of "The Fallen Dragoon" his comrades considered a classic:

Riflemen, shoot me a fancy shot,
  Straight at the heart of yon prowling vidette;
Ring me a ball on the glittering spot
  That shines on his breast like an amulet.

And Connor needed no urging, for song was a necessary part of his daily existence.

One afternoon a hack drew up in front of Menger's and a tired man alighted, worn and dusty as a foot soldier after an all-day march. He entered the hotel and signed the name "William Thompson" to the register.

Shelby was sitting on the balcony and the light of recognition flickered across his face. He called down to Jake Connor. "Get your band together, Lieutenant."

"For what, General?"

"For a serenade."

"A serenade to whom?"

"No matter, but a serenade just the same. Order, also as you go out by headquarters, that all the men not on duty, get under arms immediately and parade in front of the balcony."

As the sun set over the low hills which lay westward beyond the San Antonio River, the soldiers marched up in front of the hotel and stopped in formation. Jake Connor's band took its position under the balcony. Shelby pointed up at the window of the room to which the man had gone. "Play 'Hail to the Chief'," he said.

The band responded, but the window blinds remained drawn.

"Try 'Dixie,' boys. If the old man were dead it would bring him to life again."

But there was still no movement at the window.

"That old man up there is Kirby Smith; I would know him among a thousand. Shout for him until you are hoarse."

Then the great roar came, strong, tempestuous, welling through the streets. Finally General Kirby Smith appeared, "a look full of eagerness and wonderment on his weary and saddened face." He could not understand the ovation. Had not his officers turned against him at Marshall? Had he not been threatened by civilians all the way from Shreveport? And now the ex-soldiers of his department were cheering and yelling his name. It was impossible.

Shelby made a short speech, perhaps the only sentimental speech he ever made. The soldiers yelled and cheered again. The old general tried to reply, but could not; his men had forgiven him his faults and weaknesses.

During those days in San Antonio Shelby's camp was filled with ex-Confederates who wanted to join his force. The ranks swelled and when the Brigade left San Antonio for Eagle Pass it numbered nearly a thousand men.

One of the new recruits was an Englishman, a man of mystery and an enigma. He was middle-aged, refined in his tastes and habits, obviously had considerable means, was an elegant and accomplished linguist, had traveled over much of the world, and had an amazing knowledge of all branches of science. He was a professional soldier who had seen service with the British in the Crimea and with the French in Algeria before he had joined the forces of the Confederacy. The name he had given was obviously fictitious. Some men thought him crazy; certainly he was peculiar. He had novel, though logically explained, ideas upon suicide. He had an over-powering desire to be in a train wreck, to be in a real, first-class collision where he could observe the reactions of the injured and uninjured, if he lived; but perhaps he would be killed—it mattered not, he would run the risk. He had traveled over two continents pursuing the phantom, which had always eluded him—wrecks before him, wrecks behind him; but he had never so much as seen even an engine derailed. He enrolled as a private. He was a good soldier, became a favorite of the men, and later died at the Battle of the Sabinas River in northern Mexico.

As the new enlistees were enrolled, they were assigned to under-manned companies. Vigorous training was necessary, for many of the recruits had served in the infantry and even those

who had been cavalrymen were not accustomed to the sometimes unorthodox maneuverings which Shelby had used with
such brilliant success during the fighting in Missouri and Arkansas.

So the few days passed with constant garrison and labor details, guard and town patrol duty, rigorous training—individually,
by squads, by platoons, by companies. Arms, ammunition,
equipment and supplies were checked and packed in the wagons.
The guns of the battery were overhauled. Axles and fifth-wheels
of the vehicles were greased. Discipline was tightened. Shelby
was getting ready to move.

Then one morning the men stood reveille earlier than usual,
long before daylight. The mounts were fed and watered, and
equipment and supplies inspected. Ex-Confederates who were to
accompany the expedition rode out from San Antonio with their
belongings, which most of them carried in large, roomy saddlebags. Groups of the town's citizens joined them. They watched
the final preparations.

Then Martin Kritzer blew a blast on his bugle and the men
stood to horse.

"Prepare to mount."

The men snapped to attention, then into position.

"Mount."

A thousand men rose into their saddles.

"Troop attention." The command ran down the long lines of
horsemen. There they sat, stiffly rigid and erect, a row of
statues.

"By column of fours." Shelby's voice carried along the ranks,
stern and hard, remindful of other days.

"At a trot. Forward—Ho."

Following the point, the Brigade moved off, forded the river,
passed the old home of Antonio Navarro, who had signed the
Texas Declaration of Independence, and the old Mexican re-
doubt, crossed San Pedro Creek, and headed out on the old
Upper Presidio del Rio Grande Road. Beyond lay the low,
mesquite-covered hills which rolled away toward Castroville.

At the head of the column flew the battle-scarred Stars and
Bars of the Confederacy, and with it the guidon of the Old
Iron Brigade.

8. The March Across Southern Texas

THE ROAD forked at the Leon Creek Crossing ten miles west of San Antonio, where Upper Presidio del Rio Grande Road turned off toward the southwest while the Wells Road continued straight west to Castroville. From Castroville it angled northwest to Nandenburg, then southwest to Uvalde and Fort Inge and on to Eagle Pass. Until Uvalde was reached, the road rimmed the southern slopes of the hill country; southward from Uvalde it meandered through endless stretches of slightly-rolling, brush-covered lands and sparsely-watered, short-grass prairies.

It was a wild, arid land, with only a few small settlements and abandoned army posts to break the monotony of its emptiness. It was a country of guerrillas who had fled the war and who slept by day and raided and devoured by night. These bands hung like a threatening cloud upon the rear and flanks of the Brigade, waiting for stragglers and for the unguarded moment when they could sweep in and by surprise, rather than the sabre or revolver, carry off supplies and steal horses.

Late one night D. A. Williams and a troop of ten men ran into one of these raiding parties, a band headed by a certain "Captain" Bradford. Bradford had over thirty men and he was particularly interested in Williams' mounts and pack mules; he carefully and cunningly planned his ambuscade. Along the right of the road was a dense thicket of mesquite and behind it twisted a wide, shallow prairie stream, the sides of which were flanked by broad patches of sand. The ambush was planned for the point where the road crossed the stream.

Williams and his men had seen nothing that night to arouse suspicion and they were riding carelessly along thinking of long distant but more pleasant nights. But from long force of wartime habit, a scout ranged back and forth ahead of the slowly-moving column. George Cruzen was young in years but old and experienced in night marches and ambuscades; he knew the business of scouting.

Suddenly, off to the right, he heard a horse neigh. He slowly and carefully rode into the shadows of the mesquite and chaparral, dismounted and tied his mount. Worming his way through the undergrowth, he reached the crossing. Below him he saw the raiders, with rifles fixed, crouching in the moonlight. Returning to his horse, he galloped back to where Williams had halted the troop for a rest stop. Cruzen briefly described the location and situation of the ambush.

Williams dismounted his men, who tied their horses in the shadows. Taking only their revolvers, they moved slowly and carefully toward the left flank of the marauders. They were within a few paces when they were discovered, but fell flat on the ground just as a volley exploded in their faces.

The old Rebel yell rang out as they charged. The work was wild and bloody. When it was finished Williams had lost three men, had had two more mortally wounded, but had accounted for twenty-seven of the banditti. Henceforth the guerrillas carefully avoided contact with Shelby and his cavalrymen.

The day following the attempted ambush as the Brigade was enjoying the noon halt, James Kirtley and James Rudd rode furiously into camp. They had been operating as scouts in the rear of the column, ranging back and forth in broad, sweeping arcs, for it had been rumored that a force of Federal cavalry was attempting to cut them off from Eagle Pass. They reported that a Union detachment of about three thousand men, with a six-gun battery, was moving swiftly up behind them.

"Who commands?" asked Shelby.

"Colonel Johnson," replied Rudd.

"How far in the rear did you see him?"

"About seventeen miles."

"Mount your horse again, Rudd, you and Kirtley, and await further orders."

Shelby then called over his old ordnance master and one-time adjutant, Major James Moreland. Moreland was one of the more glittering knights errant of the Old Brigade—courtly and polite, clad in a new, gold lace-trimmed uniform, a man who was always ready for any frolic or any adventure.

"I believe," said Shelby, "you can turn the prettiest period, make the grandest bow, pay the handsomest compliment, and drink the pleasantest toast of any man in my command."

And Moreland probably clicked his heels, smartly saluted, and bowed from the waist.

"Take these two soldiers with you, ride to the rear seventeen miles, seek an interview with Colonel Johnson, and give him this."

Shelby handed him the communication which John Edwards had just finished writing.

Colonel:

My scouts inform me that you have about three thousand men, and that you are looking for me. I have only one thousand men, and yet I should like to make your acquaintance. I will probably march from my present camp about ten miles further to-day, halting on the high road between San Antonio and Eagle Pass. Should you desire to pay me a visit, you will find me at home until day after tomorrow.

Moreland took the message and galloped off, found the Federals, delivered the message with his accustomed graceful manner and complimentary words, and was received by Colonel Johnson with all the courtesy of a wartime adversary. That night Johnson camped about five miles to the rear of Shelby's column.

Shelby made preparations for a fight, but Johnson did not attack. Once afterward Johnson feinted as though to offer battle but at the last moment withdrew his men. These were the last maneuverings of the Civil War, some three weeks after the last Confederate armies had been surrendered.

Colonel Johnson was right in not attempting to prevent Shelby's crossing the Rio Grande into Mexico or to capture his force. Perhaps he had specific orders only to trail and worry Shelby. If this were true, perhaps, like Shelby, he chafed at the restraint and hoped for battle. But the war was over and it would have been useless and to no good purpose to have spilled additional blood upon the plains of south Texas.

Shelby moved leisurely on toward Eagle Pass. He crossed the Rio Medina, a clear, shallow little stream twisting between two broad flats of quicksand, passed through Castroville and the little village of Quihi. At Nandenburg, he turned southwest and paralleled the rugged hills which sloped upward to the high Texas tableland, which in turn slanted northward to the still-higher and waterless region of the dreaded *Llano Estacado*.

The Brigade reached Sabinal, a group of generally abandoned buildings, the forgotten relic of a temporary army post of the 1850's, then Uvalde, which had been named in honor of the old Spanish military leader, Don Juan de Ugalde, who had defeated the Apaches there back in the 1790's.

The route now wound through a country where greasewood, huajillo, cenizo, catclaw, sotol, and Spanish dagger were abundant. Though it was late in the season the ash-colored cenizos were filled with blossoms ranging from lavender to deep, dark purple, while the center spikes of the sotols, the roots of which were used by Mexicans to make soap and a type of fiery liquor, were rapidly pushing upward.

By this time the pattern of the day and the march were well set. Reveille was before daybreak. The men tumbled out from their blankets and slapped their arms and did jigs to restore circulation to muscles stiffened by sound slumber. Breakfast over, the mounts were fed and saddled and camp was broken.

Then the sound of Kritzer's bugle bit the morning air. The Non-coms yelled, "Fall out," and the companies quickly formed. The present or accounted-fors were called by the corporals and reported by the sergeants to the captains. Saddles creaked as cinches were tightened and saddlebags slapped on and there was the jangle of gear and the ill-humored wheezing and sneezing of horses. Kritzer blew "Boots and Saddles," and the men stood to horse. The command "prepare to mount" rang out; then "mount," and hands tipped the saddles and legs swung over; "attention," and the rows of backs straightened. "Forward at the walk—Ho," and the Brigade moved off.

The road they followed was usually only a wagon trail, remindful of the traffic of old Spanish and Republic of Texas years and of the trade which had developed since the beginning of the war. The grass was short and thin and little puffs of dust slowly ascended and merged in a steady, tenuous cloud.

There was no sound on the prairie except the constant whine of the wind, which was cool, and sometimes even cold, at night but which was the constant fanning of a furnace during the late June days. Nor were there signs of life during the day except occasional snakes and scattered prairie dog towns, with their low, entrance mounds occupied by barking, highly suspicious little fat marmonts.

The Brigade halted at noon. The men dismounted and made coffee, which was settled with hot coals, while the horses grazed over the nearly barren land. Men hunkered around their mesquite or buffalo-chip fires, smoked their pipes and cigars, and talked lazily of old raids and battles, adventures back in Austin or in San Antonio or even more sentimental memories of days before the war. The noon halts were never noisy—the low talk of the men, the uneasy stamp of the horses if they were tightly bunched, and the constant, low hum of the prairie wind.

The afternoon march was the longest. Man and beast sweated, ate dust, and craved cool water. The men hated the great emptiness of the land, the land of long horizons, the land that was south Texas, for they were hill country men and had lived in the Ozark region or in the little valleys which ran toward the wide Missouri. The afternoons were times of cursing, cursing everything connected with the expedition or the Brigade, including the officers. But a cursing, grumbling company is a fighting company, so officers smiled resignedly and took no offense.

The endless, rolling plains off to the left of the line of march shimmered under the heat haze as the afternoon wore on, while the men daydreamed on their horses of the country north of San Antonio, of live oaks and cottonwoods all in thick leaf, of grass that grew tender and fresh and seemed to blend into the pale blue of the sky, of black-eyed Susan and bluebonnet and lavender verbena which splashed the hills with color. But the rolling plains were thicketed here and there with prickly pear, whose thorns were not yet hard and whose waxy blossoms flared brightly yellow around the edges of the oval-shaped, heavy, green leaves. The rising hill country off to the northward was mantled in subdued colors and as the day began to wane the grays turned to blues, then to purples, and finally the purples deepened into even darker shades.

The pace was not hurried—trot, walk, trot, walk. But trotting gets into the insides of a man even though he is used to riding. It is a jolting, tearing gait and as the hours pass the muscles of the legs grow tired of easing the jolts, and the skin of the rump warms up with the heat and the friction to remind the rider that it is still there, and the muscles at the back of the neck complain and the torso sinews finally sound off that they are just plain tired. But trotting is the way to cover ground and at the same time save the mount in order that he may not give out after a few days of marching. Galloping and walking, or running and walking, is all right for short distances but the trot is the way to eat up the miles—forty or even fifty miles a day—and save the horse; for the experienced cavalry horse relaxes his shoulders and legs and seems simply to slap his hoofs over the ground almost of their own weight. So the pace was kept and horses and men did not suffer.

The advance scouts reported on the night's camp site, usually in the low valley of a small stream. At last they reached a rise overlooking the broken, sometimes rugged depression, with its interspersing patches of grass and brush and timber. As they rode down the slopes the fresh, clean smell of scrub cedars mingled with the harsher smell of the dry dust; and the wild, keen odor of the sagebrush asserted itself against the more subtle perfumes of the valley's hills.

The men came to life as they made the night camp—snatches of song, laughter, jokes and pranks, and occasionally a wild, Rebel yell—for the heat and sweat and dust of the day's march were quickly forgotten. The mounts were watered, fed and turned out to graze under watchful eyes of circling horse guards. Camp fires were lighted and soon the odors of cooking food commingled with the fresh, clean smell of the water and the bank-growing trees and shrubs.

Supper over, blankets were spread and the men lounged with their cigars and pipes. Here was a group surrounding a guitar-playing old ex-Missouri-Kansas guerrilla, there a cluster listening to a loud-talking, gesturing storyteller, over yonder the officers discussing the next day's march, here a fire-lit platoon singing melancholy, minor-keyed, cattle songs of the Texas prairies. As beautiful as the Swedish cattle-calls or the Swiss *Ranz des Vaches,* they consisted of chanted words in well-defined cadence, and ended with long yodels which slipped easily into high-pitched cowboy yells:

Going away to leave you,
    Ah--a--a--a--
Going away to leave you,
    Ah--a--a--a--
Going away to-morrow,

    Ah--a--a--a--
Going away to-morrow,
    Ah--a--a--a--
Never more to see you,
    Ah--a--a--a--
Never more to see you,
    Ah--a--a--a--

There was an affecting moment of silence as the yells and yodels died mournfully away and merged into the empty darkness of the night.

Over near headquarters where the guidon hung limply from its staff, sat John Edwards, carefully writing his notes. After his return from Mexico he would become one of the great editors of the nation and would write two books about the Old Brigade's record in the war and this expedition into the land south of the Rio Grande. Near him sat Shelby, poring over his maps or talking with one of the ex-Confederate civil officials.

As the men walked leisurely about the camp, it took little more than a glance to distinguish officers from enlisted men. There was a difference in their carriage. The enlisted men were stiff and walked with a definite deliberateness; officers moved with a certain carelessness and a certain sureness. The enlisted man got his attitude from the constant drill, the standing at attention and the saluting of his superiors. And the officers? Well, the old system, the old *esprit,* though not as strong as in regular armies, was present and left its mark.

The camp quieted for the night. Guards and pickets were posted. The men rolled into their blankets, feet to little fires if the night was chilly or cold. Night birds began their singing or raucous squawking. The wind hummed down the valley and mingled its sounds with the gurgling of the stream. Soon snores issued from the shadowy mounds that were sleeping men. Off in the distance a lone coyote, who sounded as though he had a hundred companions, yapped and howled and quarreled with the wind and with other feathered or footed voices of the night.

Thus, day faded into day. The pattern was set. It would so continue until the City of Mexico was reached.

One day the expedition passed a small village which had been plundered by a band of some three hundred renegades—a motley crew composed of Mexicans, deserters from both North and South, desperate fugitives from the justice of many states, half-breeds and full-blooded Indians, mountain and desert men from New Mexico, Arizona, Colorado and as far away as California. The outlaws had fled toward their fortified hideout set high in a pattern of rugged hills about twenty miles distant.

The villagers asked Shelby for assistance to recover their stolen property. Responding to their appeal, he assigned the mission to Alonzo Slayback, colonel of a regiment in the Old Brigade, and an eloquent, hard-riding Cossack.

Taking with him two hundred volunteers, Slayback set out for the citadel of the banditti and caught up with the raiders just before they reached their fort. No command was needed by the veterans, who charged with a furious rush, revolvers ready. But for the broken character of the ground the attack would have become an extermination. Slayback returned with the stolen goods without having lost a single man.

During the march from San Antonio to Eagle Pass three men came into Shelby's camp and represented themselves as having been soldiers in Lee's army, now on their way to Mexico. They had never been in Texas and knew nothing of Mexico and felt it would be safer if they joined Shelby's forces. They were enrolled and assigned to one of the companies.

Some days later it was noticed that they were at least partially familiar with the Spanish language, a peculiar circumstance since men from the eastern part of the South were usually unacquainted with Spanish. Doubts began to be cast at the truth of their former statements and a careful watch was kept on them. Later they were to be the cause of a tragic incident in Piedras Negras.

When the expedition was within two or three days' march of the Rio Grande, General Kirby Smith expressed a desire to precede the Brigade into Mexico and asked for a mounted escort to hurry him to the border. Shelby willingly agreed and Langhorne received the honor of convoying his former commander-in-chief to the Rio Grande. With Smith went several former Confederate officers and civilians who either had contacts or connections in Piedras Negras or Monterrey, or who were tired of the slow, organized march and the strict military regulations of the Brigade. Some of them Shelby would not see again, some he would find in Monterrey or in the City of Mexico. Other civilians and former officers, however, including Governor Reynolds, continued with the expedition as far as Monterrey.

Langhorne conveyed the party to Eagle Pass. After bidding him farewell, Smith said: "With an army of such soldiers as Shelby has, and this last sad act in the drama of exile would have been left unrecorded." Langhorne did not argue the statement, but, along with some of his men, he must have wondered: "And with a leader such as Shelby, this last sad act in the drama of exile would have been left unrecorded."

So the Nueces River was crossed, and Turkey Creek and Elm Creek. The expedition drew nearer the Rio Grande and at last came in sight of the old village which the Mexicans called El Paso del Aguila, the Pass of the Eagle, so named because in the early days an eagle had made daily flights back and forth across the river to its nest in a large cottonwood tree on the Mexican bank. Passing Fort Duncan, an abandoned post which had been built in the 1850's and garrisoned during the early part of the Civil War by the Confederates, the Brigade moved down the east bank of the Rio Grande about two miles to Eagle Pass.

The southern boundary of the former Confederate States of America had been reached. The last scene in the drama of the American Civil War was about to be enacted.

9. The Fallen Flag

THE SQUALID, dusty border town of Eagle Pass lay atop a low bluff on the Texas side of the Rio Grande; the Mexican village of Piedras Negras, the place of the black stones, lay on the other. Between them flowed the sand-banked and bottomed stream, at this point of considerable width and depth, the stream which Mexicans called (and still call) the Rio Bravo del Norte, the Brave River of the North. Since colonial days the two villages had been mildly prosperous for they were the exchange place of goods of south Texas and the Mexican Saluria district, areas in themselves too poor to produce towns of any real importance.

The old river ford had witnessed stirring events through the years. Apache and Lipan Indians had originally used the crossing. Here Mexican and Spanish settlers had crossed the river to claim land grants on the north side of the Rio Grande. Here Americans had forded during the Mexican War for Independence from Spain in the early years of the century—Americans on their way to Guanajuato and Dolores Hidalgo and even Guadalajara to join the Mexican Revolutionaries—Americans from all the American states, from as far north as Maine—Americans whose sacrifices have been forgotten on the pages of both Mexican and American history.

The ford had been used by '49ers on their way to distant California by the north Mexican route. It had been used by American soldiers and Mexican raiding parties during the War with Mexico in the 1840's. Here, too, Captain James Callahan of the American Army had crossed on his way to attack the Lipan Indians in 1855, an expedition which had caused complications between the United States and Mexico, for Callahan had fought a battle with the Mexicans, had been chased out of Mexico by Captain Menchaca of the Mexican Army, burning Piedras Negras before retreating to safety across the Rio.

During the Civil War Eagle Pass was an active town, for through it passed vast quantities of cotton on the way to Mexican Gulf ports and contraband goods from France and England on the way to the Confederacy. The town also served as an outlet for the escape of numerous German and other citizens of Texas who were anti-secessionists. After the withdrawal of the Confederate garrison at Fort Duncan, the entire region became the headquarters of "evasionists," who escaped Confederate military service, and "bushwhackers," "skulkers," and other lawless characters who marauded and raided and killed. The end of the war had suddenly stopped commercial and trading activity and at the time of Shelby's arrival, Eagle Pass was a dead town, plagued by the lawless bands which roamed the thinly-settled plains of South Texas from the Big Bend of the Rio Grande to Matamoras and northward to San Antonio and Galveston.

Shelby passed through the town and bivouacked, set up his artillery in battery bearing upon the Mexican shore, posted guards and pickets, and went serenely and comfortably into camp.

Across the river, Governor Andres Viesca, Commandant at Piedras Negras and Juarista governor of the Mexican state of Coahuila, and his staff watched the proceedings with mixed feelings. Viesca felt fairly safe with two thousand soldiers at his back, but he carefully watched Shelby's column debouch from the plateau and go into camp above the river. He saw the artillery planted and noticed that the guns were pointed toward Piedras Negras and that they commanded the town. He saw trained, march-dusty cavalrymen go efficiently about the business of their camp duties. Viesca knew that Benito Juarez was supported by the government of the United States, but he also knew that the Confederate States of America had been flirting with Emperor Maximilian. And this force flew the Stars and Bars.

All of the small ferry boats seemed to be on the Mexican side of the river, and on that side all was quiet. The boats did not return and the boatmen withdrew into the town.

"Who can speak Spanish?" asked Shelby.

One man spoke up that he could speak the language, a man who had joined the Brigade at Corsicana, about whom nothing was known and whose name was obviously fictitious, a man who said that he had been in Mexico.

"Can you swim?" queried Shelby.

"Well?"

"Suppose you try for a skiff, that we may open negotiations with the town."

"I dare not. I am afraid to go over alone."

Shelby had known fear in battle and he knew that his men had known it, but both he and his men had conquered that gnawing, empty feeling that steals through the throat and down into the stomach of all soldiers when danger is present, when the future is unknown but is certain to be dark and bloody. Good and experienced soldiers have conquered that fear, but it is always there, ever present, though never admitted until after the incident has passed.

"*Afraid!*" The words were uttered in tones of half pity, half contempt. "Then stand aside."

His voice rang out. A job needed doing.

"Volunteers for the venture—swimmers to the front."

65

Full fifty men strode forward.

He chose but two, then turned to Dick Collins, the battery commander.

"Load with canister. If a hair of their heads is hurt, not one stone upon another shall be left in Piedras Negras."

George Winship and Dick Berry plunged into the water. Here was but one more battle hazard. They had faced enemy bullets on many a wild charge and in many a foray. They would take their chances with the waves of a river.

They crossed and brought back one of the boats. Meanwhile, Colonel Frank Gordon, who had put the 9th Wisconsin to flight at the First Newtonia, had selected twenty-five men to accompany him across the river with a flag of truce.

While these preparations were being made a skiff put off from the Mexican side bearing two men under a white flag. Shelby's frowning cannon had caused Governor Viesca to expect a quick bombardment of Piedras Negras. He asked for time to remove the women and children.

Gordon crossed the river, disembarked, and proceeded to the main plaza. Viesca rode into the square, surrounded by his staff, and received Gordon with all the pomp and circumstance at his disposal. The polished and elegant Viesca, who was half governor and half military commander, was typical of his class and station, was eloquent of speech and gesture, but extremely careful in his statements and guarantees of friendship. He would talk only with Shelby, so later in the day Shelby crossed the river and had a conference with Governor Viesca. The meetings between the two men continued for two days, two days of arguments and counter arguments, wrangling over details and arrangements. Shelby was outspoken, blunt, abrupt, and sometimes haughty and suspicious; Viesca was gracious, voluble, suave, and magnificent in promises, offers, and inducements.

Governor Viesca's proposal was tailor-made for Shelby's general plan for he offered Shelby and his brigade service with President Benito Juarez. Shelby would be given military control over the states of Nuevo Leon, Coahuila and Tamaulipas, while Viesca retained the civil authority. Viesca suggested that Shelby make his headquarters at Piedras Negras until such time as he could create a sizable army, then march upon Monterrey, which

Frontier cotton press at Piedras Negras, 1864.

was held by the French forces of Emperor Maximilian. The plan was an attractive one. Shelby had dreamed of an empire beyond the Rio Grande, an empire where the ex-Confederate could create a new Southland, where military fame would be gained and the promises of adventure were unlimited. He would enlist twenty thousand men and with such a force at his back would have no difficulty in conquering and occupying all of Northern Mexico.

After the final conference, Shelby recrossed the river to present the plan to his men. The meeting was long and the arguments earnestly and resolutely presented. Shelby waxed eloquent perhaps, for here was a new empire lying at hand across the river.

"If you are all of my mind, boys, and will take your chances along with me, it is Juarez and the Republic from this on until we die here, one by one, or win a kingdom. We have the nucleus of a fine army—we have cannon, muskets, ammuni-

67

tion, some good prospects for recruits, a way open to Sonora, and according to the faith that is in us will be the measure of our loss or victory."

The men listened, intent and sober.

"Determine for yourselves. You know Viesca's offer. What he fails to perform we will perform for ourselves, so that when the game is played out there will be scant laughter over any Americans trapped or slain by treachery."

After considerable general discussion, Colonel Ben Elliott arose; Elliott, who had been with the Old Brigade, who had been wounded four times, and who had worked his way up to a colonelcy; Elliott, well-trained and proud, a Virginia Military Institute graduate, the tall, grim Saul who seldom smiled, who was always deadly serious. Elliott was the spokesman for the men.

"General, if you order it, we will follow you into the Pacific Ocean; but we are all Imperialists, and would prefer service under Maximilian."

This was a stunning blow to Shelby, for his plans had been focused toward Juarez and the Mexican Republic. He well knew the romantic and chivalrous nature of his men. The romantic appeal of the Mexican Empire and the Empress Carlota had been too strong. But they were enlisting in another Lost Cause, a cause which had been doomed to failure from the beginning. These reflections took but a moment.

"Is this your answer, men?"

"It is." There was not a waver in Elliott's voice. The men nodded agreement.

"Then it is mine, too. Henceforth we will fight under Maximilian. Tomorrow, at four o'clock in the afternoon, the march shall commence for Monterrey."

Shelby paused.

"Let no man repine. You have chosen the Empire, and, perhaps, it is well, but bad or good, your fate shall be my fate, and your fortune my fortune."

As Shelby left the meeting he remarked: "Poor, proud fellows—it is principle with them, and they had rather starve under the Empire than feast in a republic. Lucky, indeed, for many of them if to famine there is not added a fusillade." Those were Shelby's words as John Edwards later reported them.

Thus Shelby's dream ended, the dream of gathering a strong force from all parts of a reunited North and South and marching into Mexico to the relief of Juarez. But during the past four years, Shelby and Edwards, his adjutant, had fashioned the men of the Iron Brigade into a group of knights and crusaders fighting for fair ladies and a holy cause. Shelby had been a dynamic battle commander who had fired the young men of Missouri and Arkansas who followed him and he had a genius for doing the dramatic thing at the dramatic time.

So when the vote was taken at Eagle Pass, the men who had been living in a heroic, though bloody fantasy were willing to gamble on a bloody, unrealistic future rather than on a more realistic opportunity, in order to continue their supposed heroics by marching into a foreign country not in the cause of democracy but in the cause of kings and queens, to attempt to rescue an already dying empire. It was heroic, magnificent, but it was not sound, considered judgment.

The clock had been moved backward two hundred years. One could see the battle uniforms (when they could be secured), with gold braid and silver ornamentation—the ring tournaments when in camp—all the stately courtesies to ladies and to gentlemen—the doffing of hats to wounded enemy officers—the black plumes and blood-red sumac sprigs in the hatband— champions who fought before watching armies—the gaily caparisoned horses—the brilliant parade before the bloody charge— the raising of hats to the enemy before battle—the bows and the shouts of *"en garde," "en avant,"* and other such phrases of bygone, knightly days.

One could almost envision the field of Naseby—the wild and daring charge of Prince Rupert's horse which carried everything before it and beyond the main body of the army, Cromwell's troops reining in, restoring the balance of the action and facing about toward Rupert's tired cavaliers; the last, final effort of King Charles as he sent his men forward with a cheer, "one charge more, gentlemen, and the day is ours"; the hour afterward, when his last regiment was broken and his army had ceased to exist, and the King, himself, a fugitive.

To many of the Old Brigade the war had been bucklered

Cavalier against iron-pot headed Puritan, patrician against plebeian, noble against commoner, knight against armed serf.

But the last page in this heroic volume of a sometimes mythical, sometimes living chivalric South was about to be turned; it was turned and the book was closed the next morning, the morning of July the fourth.

Shelby drew up his Brigade in dress parade front on the banks of the Rio Grande. Before it floated the Confederate flag, a banner which two years before had been presented to the Brigade by the women of a small Arkansas town. The town's newspaper had reported the speech of acceptance of Major John Edwards, acting for General Jo Shelby:

"Made by the fair hands of women; dedicated to a grand and glorious cause; sanctified by the holy symbols of a true faith—its crest to-day is as bright as the sunlight that flashes on steel. Pure and stainless as an angel-guarded child, it must never be dishonored. It is confided to your keeping as a tender and timid maiden gives her virgin heart to the first sweet whisperings of love. Cherish it, protect it, fight for it, die for it. There is a day to come when it must receive its baptism of fire and blood in the rattle of discordant musketry, and the thunder of impatient drums. Let it ever be on the crest of battle, its blue folds the meteor of the storm, its bright associations cheering the warrior's heart like the white plume of Navarre."

Edwards, who wrote with a grandiloquent pen, was not an orator—but he had memorized his written words and had delivered them well.

He closed: "When the deadly war is over; when the red banners of strife have gleamed over the last foughten field, and paled beyond the sunset shore; when our glorious cause has risen beautiful from its urn of death and chamber of decay, with the eternal sunlight of land redeemed on its wings; and the white opinions of peace, like a brooding dove, are hovering above us, let the memories of this day go with you; let the affections of your hearts go with this old banner—all tattered and torn though it may be—and cling to it, and linger round it, like the dew on a summer hill."

Now the old banner flew above a New Brigade, standing at attention on the banks of a distant stream. Colonels Ben Elliott, D. A. Williams, Frank Gordon, Alonzo Slayback, and Yandell Blackwell came forward and took the flag.

As Edwards later wrote: "The old tattered battle-flag of the division was brought from its resting-place and given once more to the winds. Rent and bruised, and crimson with the blood of heroes—it had never been dishonored. Missouri breezes had felt the flapping of its silken folds; woman's imperial hand had decorated it with battle-mottoes; sweet, coy victory—her locks heavy with the dust of conflicts and red with the blood of martyrs—had caressed it often and tenderly; ambition had plumed it with the royal crest of triumph; fate and dear dauntless hearts had borne it flashing like a meteor upon the rough, stormy waves of battle waters; shining like the face of a struggling king, it had gleamed grandly through the smoke and the sorrow of two hundred desperate fields; and broad bared now, and worn, and old—it was displayed once more to its followers before the swift waves of the Rio Grande closed over it forever."

The five colonels held it up for a few brief moments, then weighted it, and waded far out into the river. Gently, they lowered it into the water.

Overcome by a sudden burst of emotion, Shelby tore the black plume from his hat and cast it into the river, while tears ran unashamedly down the cheeks of his battle-tried veterans.

Colonel Alonzo Slayback composed the requiem of the buried banner, which closes:

> They buried then that flag and plume in the
> River's rushing tide,
> Ere that gallant few
> Of the tried and true
> Had been scattered far and wide.
> And that group of Missouri's valiant throng,
> Who had fought for the weak against the strong—
> Who had charged and bled
> Where Shelby led,
> Were the last who held above the wave
> The glorious flag of the vanquished brave,
> No more to rise from its watery grave!

Slayback's verses are crude doggerel, but they reveal the sorrow and the glory of a defeated cause; he was only saying, as

71

Childe Harold had said, "My native Land, good night." Perhaps he will be forgiven his lack of poetic genius for it was his flag and his country which had fallen.

The flag of the old Brigade lay at the bottom of the Rio Grande. It was the last flag to fly over an organized Confederate force. Today, the spot where it is buried is sometimes called the Grave of the Confederacy.

As the expedition moved along the river bank toward the crossing, it followed the guidon of the Old Brigade, a ragged, battle-scarred streamer which would lead it to Monterrey, to Saltillo, to Parras, to San Luis Potosi and Queretaro—and on to the fabled old City of the Palaces, the Imperial Capital of Maximilian, the City of Mexico.

IV

THE ROAD TO
MONTERREY

10. Piedras Negras

THE BRIGADE CROSSED THE river and went into camp at the edge of Piedras Negras. After guards had been posted, the wagon train, the battery, ammunition and supplies were brought over, and the men spent the rest of the day lounging about camp or walking through the town.

The next morning Shelby and his staff visited Governor Viesca to inform him of the new turn of events. Viesca was stunned when informed of the decision. He had happily gone to bed the night before in the satisfied belief that he had secured a great *coup d'etat* for Juarez and the Liberal Cause; now the fantasy had ended—would Shelby, now that he had decided for the Empire, attack and try to occupy northern Mexico. Viesca was not particularly worried but he would be cautious.

He possessed all the nonchalance of his nationality. When the Mexican has run his race and is face to face with the inevitable, he becomes stolidly indifferent—if he faces a firing squad, he calmly mutters an *"adios"* to friends and loved ones, rolls and takes a few puffs from his *cigarillo,* quickly makes peace with his God and with his conscience, folds his arms across his chest and bows to his executioners. So it was with Viesca. What was done was done. God had willed it. *Vaya con Dios,* go with God.

Something, however, might be salvaged from the misfortune. Shelby had an immense wagon train, loaded with supplies of every description. He had a tremendous number of late-model rifles and plenty of ammunition. He had a fine battery of artillery. Here was the opportunity for some successful bargaining, if it could be done with finesse and delicate discrimination.

Shelby informed him that the Brigade would move to Monterrey to join the French forces there and Viesca replied that there were two alternate routes. He could go by way of Gigedo, Astillero, Candela, Alamo Mocho, and Castannela to Saltillo, and from there to Monterrey; or, he could travel to Gigedo, then to Lampazos, and on to Monterrey via Beneventura and Naria. The road over the first route was passable for the wagons and artillery, but the Juaristas had a strong army in the area to oppose his progress. On the other hand, the region of the second route was controlled by neither the Juaristas nor the forces of the Emperor and it was a land filled with armed bandits and Lipan Indians, and the road was impassable for wheeled vehicles for it was little more than a trail. In either case, it would be impossible for Shelby to take his wagon train and artillery.

Shelby was aware that he could only take what could be carried in saddle bags or on pack animals and he had already decided to sell the battery and most of the supplies and small arms. He would make the best bargain he could. Negotiations began at once.

The agreement was reached after much discussion and argument. Sixteen thousand dollars in specie and another sixteen thousand in Juarez script (on which the men never collected a farthing) would be paid for the cannon, arms, ammunition and the miscellaneous supplies.

But Viesca did not have that much money in his possession, so a levy or *prestamo* would have to be collected from the citizens of Piedras Negras. The collection of *prestamos* was an old practice of Mexican revolutionaries and even governments and Viesca was a man with considerable experience; no governor would be ignorant of the most efficient methods of extracting the last possible peso. He was confident. He would have little difficulty.

Viesca's officers drew up a list of the town's merchants, traders and more affluent citizens. The sum assessed to each was placed opposite his name. An officer, backed by a squad of soldiers, called upon each of the listed men, bowed and murmured *"Buenos Dias,"* wished him and his family good health (even to uncles and cousins several times removed), named the sum which had been levied against him and waited.

Having little opportunity to choose—it was either the money

or the guardhouse and perhaps execution—the victim paid the sum, courteously bowed in return to the officer, and turned away, calling down upon the heads of all *Yanquis* all the curses of Heaven and Hell. The money was deposited in the Custom House for safekeeping.

When questioned about the wisdom of selling the artillery, guns and ammunition to the Mexicans, who vastly outnumbered him, "What is to prevent them from taking back the money and annihilating you?" Shelby replied laconically: "You seem to forget, sir, that we still have our side arms." He knew his men. He had no fears for the safety of his Brigade.

While these negotiations had been going on the men completed routine camp duties and finished their regular drill. Now they lounged about the little town, scattered in all directions, careless of possible trouble, perhaps indifferent to it. They would make the most of the opportunity.

The afternoon hours passed. Sounds of song came from *cantinas* and *tiendas,* intermingled with lusty oaths and raucous laughter, for liquors were plentiful and the soldiers were relaxing from the drudgery and danger of war.

Shelby and his men had not noticed that the three men who claimed they had been soldiers in Lee's army, and who had joined the expedition shortly before it reached Eagle Pass, had been going among the Mexican soldiers pointing out the branded horses which had been acquired in south Texas.

Branding of animals was a universal practice in both Texas and Mexico. The brand was the badge of ownership. It was also a matter of record. In case the lost or stolen horse was found, prove the brand and take the animal. It was the universal law. From it there was no appeal.

Some of the mounts had undoubtedly been stolen out of Mexico. Could their brands be proved? If not, at least here was a golden opportunity which should not be overlooked. The Mexicans had listened. Their greed won over good judgment. By the Holy Virgin, the Gringos would deliver up every horse wearing a Mexican brand—and perhaps a few which wore Texas brands.

Some distance down the street from headquarters, Ike Berry sat on his horse with one leg thrown over the saddle horn, idly smoking. Around him were tied several branded animals,

75

those belonging to Kirtley, Chiles, Rudd, Yowell, Armistead, and a few others. Berry did not notice the handsome young Mexican officer who approached with thirty soldiers at his back, accompanied by the three renegade Americans, but Jim Wood, who was lounging at the door of one of the cafes, noticed the party and he turned to Martin Kritzer:

"They are in skirmishing order. Old Jo has delivered the arms; it may be we shall take them back again."

The party reached the vicinity of Ike Berry and one of the Americans went straight up to him and took hold of the horse's bridle. Berry knew the man. He spoke cheerily to him.

"How now, comrade?"

"This is my horse; he wears my brand; I have followed him to Mexico. Dismount!"

Berry smiled down at him while long, white wreathes of smoke curled up from the bowl of the meerschaum. Then he slowly and carefully knocked the ashes from his pipe, gradually moving, as he did so, his foot back into the stirrup. Gradually his expression changed. The friendly smile faded and changed into the terrible hardness of the old battle-smile. His comrades, who were observing the action, knew from long association with him that the swift, horrible movement would soon come and that it would leave a dead or desperately wounded man upon the street.

Then he suddenly rose in the saddle. The heavy cavalry sabre came from its saddle-scabbard, described a broad arc in the air, and descended. With its falling the man's arm fell away, cut clean at the shoulder, while blood spouted from the stump with every heart beat. The man fell and threshed upon the ground.

With a yell, the Mexican soldiers fanned out and surrounded the fourteen or fifteen men. Yowell broke through their ranks and ran to the *cantina* where Shelby sat drinking cognac and talking with the Englishman.

"What is it?" he asked Yowell.

"They are after the horses."

"What horses?"

"The branded horses; those obtained from the Rosser ranch."

"Ah! and after we have delivered the arms, too." He ran to the door and looked out into the street.

"The rally! The rally! Sound the rally!" Shelby yelled to Martin Kritzer, the bugler, as he rushed off toward where the Mexicans were swarming around Berry and the others. "We have eaten of their salt, and they have betrayed us; we have to come to them as friends, and they would strip us like barbarians. It is war again."

Kritzer's bugle blast swept through the streets and suddenly-sobered men rushed from the *cantinas* and cafes and swarmed into the melee. There was the sudden barking of revolvers. Jim Wood leveled down on the young captain, fired and the man threw up his arms, staggered and fell dead on his face.

With the noise of the gunfire, the entire Brigade rushed to arms, believing that Viesca had attacked them. Langhorne dashed to the Custom House and locked its sentinels in a back room. D. A. Williams swept down on the artillery and ammunition wagons, scattered the guard with a rattling fusillade, took possession and started to man the guns. Smaller parties under Kirtley, Jim Wood, Winship, Fell, and Martin Kritzer seized the boats at the river, then swept through the town which had become a maelstrom of galloping, shouting men.

The Mexican soldiers assembled and formed ranks while their drums rolled.

Shelby rode among his men, storming at them to stop firing and return to camp, but for a few minutes they were completely beyond his control.

At this critical juncture, Governor Viesca rushed into the square, his hat off, pleading in impassioned tones, apologizing for the incident, imploring his men to stop fighting.

Discipline at last triumphed and the men returned to headquarters where they formed in line, quiet, stolid, ominous. Nearby was the battery of artillery, which had been sold and then captured from the enemy. One soldier said, with grim irony, "We want to sleep to-night, and for fear of Vesuvius, we have brought the crater with us."

The work had been quick and deadly. Two of the Americans who had caused the trouble lay dead on the street, along with seventeen Mexicans; the first American, whose arm had been neatly severed, strangely enough recovered.

As night came on, an unusual quiet fell over the town. The

77

Americans went about their camp duties and the Mexican soldiers returned to their barracks. Viesca wanted his cannon back,
but he feared that the aroused and desperate Americans might
not only keep the guns but might turn them upon him. He
pled with Shelby and threatened his own men if there was any
more trouble. Shelby finally calmed down and the two men returned to the old game of diplomacy.

After supper the Americans clustered around their campfires.
Suddenly they heard a long, shrill yell that was half Mexican
cattle-call and half Indian warwhoop and instantly thronged into
the street. The yell was repeated, this time nearer, shriller, loud-
er. Tension mounted. Was a new battle in the offing?

Two soldiers came up the street dragging an unwilling victim
who was ghastly pale and whose legs refused their office. William Fell and Joe Moreland meant business, however, for one
had his revolver drawn and the other carried a naked sabre.
As they reached the first group of soldiers, Moreland shouted:
"Make way, Missourians, and therefore barbarians, for the only
living and animated specimen of the *genus* Polyglot now upon
the North American continent."

The men relaxed. Here was no trouble. Fell and Moreland
were only having some fun. They waited eagerly.

"Look at him, you heathens, and uncover yourselves. Draw
nigh to him, you savages, and fall upon your knees. Touch him,
you blood-drinkers, and make the sign of the cross."

Back went the revolvers into their holsters. The soldiers
pressed around their two comrades and the prisoner.

"What did you call him?" asked Armistead.

"A Polyglot, you Fejee Islander; a living dictionary; a human
mausoleum with the bones of fifty languages."

The captive was indeed a strange and curious individual.
Upon interrogation, the men discovered that he was a native
Louisianian and had been born in New Orleans of Creole par-
ents. He had traveled over the entire world and claimed to
speak not only English, French, and Spanish, but German,
Italian, Greek, and Arabic, as well as dozens of lesser dialects.
He claimed to have served with General E. R. S. Canby in
New Mexico, and if this were true had probably deserted when
the work became heavy or danger threatened. At the present

moment, he was serving Juarez in Piedras Negras as a collector of customs, keeper of accounts, translator, spy—literally anything that was required.

He out-Doned the Mexican Dons of Piedras Negras with his soft, persuasive tones, his grandiloquent language, and his bows and studied politeness when he finally realized that he was in no physical danger. He charmed Shelby and his men with tales of adventure, which he told in a curious mixture of tongues.

But he was an accomplished scoundrel. The next morning, when Shelby and Viesca went to the Custom House, they found that one of the bags of money was missing, a bag containing about two thousand dollars. Shelby was incredulous, Viesca waved his arms, swore, and implored the guidance of the Holy Virgin. The Polyglot only smiled and had nothing to say, offered no explanation for the loss.

With the arrival of some of Shelby's officers, the Polyglot became more articulate. Under the spell of his multilingual vocabulary and his magnetic eloquence, Shelby and his men forgot the financial loss. Here was a man, in some ways at least, after their own hearts. They yielded completely to his conversation and his charm, and when they departed presented him with a gold-decorated ivory-handled revolver.

Viesca and Shelby concluded their business. The governor paid over the money and Shelby returned the battery. The money was divided equally among officers and men and according to Thomas Westlake the shares amounted to about sixty dollars and "all were dealt fairly with."

Viesca was happy. Though considerably disappointed that the Brigade had not joined the cause of Juarez, he was thankful that it was at last about to leave Piedras Negras. His blessings for a safe journey were given with all his old pomp and graciousness.

The pack train was formed and the Brigade mounted. At a walk it filed through Piedras Negras and headed southwest toward the village of Fuente, some twelve miles distant. In an hour it reached the brow of the low line of hills that sloped upward from the Rio Grande. Here it halted. The men turned and looked behind them.

There was the valley, gently sloping down toward the river.

79

There were the two towns which lay opposite each other at the crossing and above Eagle Pass abandoned Fort Duncan. But flying from its flagpole was an old and battered Confederate flag. The banner of the Old Brigade had found its resting place in the bottom of the river, but some soldier had been unable to leave the land of the Confederacy without a flag.

The men were silent: "Some memories of home and kindred may have come then as dreams come in the night; some placid past may have outlined itself as a mirage against the clear sky of the distant north; some voice may have spoken even then to ears that heard and heeded, but the men made no sign. The bronzed faces never softened." Then the ranks closed and they moved off.

At this moment a galloping horseman bore down upon them from the direction of Piedras Negras. He rode up to Shelby, who was at the head of the column. *"Amigo,"* he said, as he shook hands.

"Friend, yes. It is a good name. Would you go with us?"

"No."

"What will you have?"

"One last word at parting."

Shelby nodded.

"Once upon a time in Texas an American was kind to me. Maybe he saved my life. I would believe so, because I want a reason for what is done between us."

"Speak out fairly, man. If you need help, tell me."

"No help, *Señor,* no money, no horses, no friendship—none of these. Only a few last words."

"What are they?"

"Beware of the Sabinas!"

11. The Battle of the Sabinas

I T W A S only thirty miles to the village of Gigedo and the road was good. The horses were rested. The excitement in Piedras Negras had made the men more eager to begin the march to Monterrey; they were impatient, excited, gay.

But Shelby held them down. It was a hundred and forty miles

to Lampazos and a hundred and twenty-five miles from there to Monterrey. The country was rough and arid, mountains had to be crossed, the road would soon become but a trail, and Lipan Indians and renegade marauders were hungry for good cavalry horses, rifles, revolvers, and the miscellany of articles carried in the well filled saddle bags. Caution and prudence must be observed. The advance, therefore, proceeded at a steady but unhurried pace.

The grassless plain stretched out before them, mesquite covered and dotted with chaparral. Dry and parched arroyos, thirsty for rain which seldom came, wound serpent-like back toward the Rio Grande. The arroyos were usually narrow watercourses but sometimes their little valleys widened and here a few water-starved, bedraggled trees, their leaves hanging limply in the air, struggled for existence. It was midsummer and the dust alternately swirled upward with the heat-filled gusts of wind or hung low like a pall.

There was a brooding lifelessness to this land; only occasionally was it broken when a lobo wolf or coyote scampered from behind a dry and withered patch of buffalo grass or a few straggling dots that were running antelope faded into the distance. But always overhead were the *zopilotes,* the buzzards, winging high and aimlessly or circling in lazy arcs around some victim of the merciless life-and-death pattern of the desert.

The night camps were the only real breaks in the monotony of the march. The column halted, the men dismounted and the horses slacked off, with hanging heads, sweat coursing down their sides in little rivulets and dripping slowly off into the dust. Man and beast rested a little and the horses were watered after they had cooled a little. After the rest came drill, for throughout the march to the City of Mexico Shelby never relaxed this old habit. They were in dangerous country and a trained company would survive where an untrained troop would be shot to pieces. The men grumbled and remarked that Old Jo, who was not a West Pointer, had an unnatural love for "the precision of the parade ground."

The horse herds were sent out under guard after the drill. Now came relaxation from the day's heat and dust. Cooking fires were lighted and kettles were soon bubbling. Pipes were brought out after supper and the men lay around the fires. Poker and other card games got under way and some of the players soon found themselves, as one of the men remarked, as clean of cash as Adam, before the Temptation, was innocent of sin. Jake Connor got out his guitar and a group gathered and began to sing sentimental songs.

Over at the camp's edge sat a cluster of men around a small fire, joking and laughing hilariously. Someone started singing "Shelby's Mule" and soon the whole camp was singing:

"Ho boys! Make a Noise!

The Yankees are afraid!

The river's up, Hell's to pay—

Shelby's on a Raid!"

It was a wild, raucous song and always ended with a still wilder Rebel Yell. Long after the war a northern soldier recalled the song: "In my day I had done some tall marching, after Jackson, Mosby, Imboden, Jenkins and other Confederate commanders in Virginia; had been startled by their bugle calls, alarmed by the Rebel Yell, but never heard anything like 'Shelby's Mule'."

Finally the camp quieted down. Camp and picket guards were posted. The outriding scouts mounted and began their silent circling. The horse guards leaned across the horns of their saddles, alert and vigilant. Overhead the full Comanche Moon, as Texans called it, hovered in the sky. Bull bats dived at full speed through the lights of the flickering campfires. Another day had ended.

One day the expedition passed a raided, burned-out village. Lipans or guerrillas, having scented the opportunity of plunder and human prey, had swept down upon it. Dead men, women and children littered the little street. There were evidences of torturing, in the perhaps vain hope of hidden treasures—men who had been hanged head down from doorways, who had been flayed alive, or whose feet had been slowly roasted over open fires. A young girl, whose body had not yet been mutilated by ants or animals, lay as if in sleep.

The men rode silently through the village, their usually rough voices hushed, but upon their faces rose that pity that would become a terrible vengeance.

82

Shelby turned to Ben Elliott, who was riding with him at the head of the column, and curtly said: "Should the worst come to the worst, keep one pistol ball for yourself, Colonel. Better suicide than a fate like this."

And back amid the troop the strange Englishman grew sterner and sadder. Hereafter then they halted he more carefully checked his arms than was his habit and gave special consideration to his mount.

Shortly before tattoo that night the guards brought two men into camp. They were deserters from the French Foreign Legion at Monterrey. They believed that death was imminent.

"Where do you go?" asked Shelby.

"To Texas."

"And why to Texas?"

"For a home; for any life other than a dog's life; for freedom, for a country." For a country? Strange words to men who had just lost a country, who were now countryless and in a foreign land.

"You are soldiers, and yet you desert?"

"We were soldiers, and yet they made robbers of us. We do not hate the Mexicans. They never harmed Austria, our country."

"Where did you cross the Sabinas?"

"At the ford upon the main road."

"Who were there and what saw you?"

"No living thing, General. Nothing but trees and rocks and water."

Shelby studied them. They probably spoke the truth. But the warning, "Beware of the Sabinas!" If the Mexicans and Lipans had laid an ambush at the crossing would they have permitted these men to have escaped across with their horses? Yes, their strategy was obvious.

The Brigade crossed the broken, rolling plain, entered the foothills of the eastern Sierra Madres. It was a wasted, dangerous country and Shelby grew more cautious as he neared the Sabinas River.

Early one afternoon the column approached the crossing. The day had been hot and dusty and long. The men were sweat-stained and tired and looked forward to a good camp site, with grass and water and sheltering trees. They were in vicious humor and therefore in superb fighting condition, a signal or a shot and they would turn into a yelling, charging horde of flame and steel.

Shelby called a halt and ordered D. A. Williams forward with twenty men. Williams rode up.

"It may be child's play or warrior's work, but whatever it is, let me know quickly."

Williams' blue eyes flashed. He knew that danger lay ahead at the crossing.

"Any further orders, General?"

"None. Try the ford and penetrate the brush beyond. If you find one rifle barrel among the trees, be sure there are five hundred close at hand. Murderers love to mass themselves."

Williams and his troop galloped off toward the river. Five minutes later the main body was put in motion, though at a slower pace. It was about an hour's ride to the crossing. Williams would have ample time to reconnoiter. Shelby called the officers up.

"You know as well as I do what is waiting for us at the river."

The men nodded.

"This side Piedras Negras a friendly Mexican spoke some words at parting, full of warning, and doubtless sincere. He at least believed in the danger, and so do I. Williams has gone forward to flush the game, if game there be."

The men were silent.

"Above and below the main road, the road we are now upon, there are fords where men might cross at ease and horses find safe and certain footing. I shall try none of them. When the battle opens, and the bugle call is heard, you will form your men in fours and follow me. The question is to gain the further bank, and after that we shall see."

Shelby paused. "One thing more before we march. Come here, Elliott."

The battle-scarred warrior leaned forward.

"You will lead the forlorn hope. It will take ten men to form it. That is enough to give up of my precious ones. Call for volunteers—for men to take the water first, and draw the first merciless fire. After that we will be in at the death."

84

Two hundred volunteered and Elliott chose his ten—Cundiff, Langhorne, Wood, Winship, Kirtley, Woods, Fell, McDougall, Rudd and Chiles. They moved out at two hundred yards ahead of the column.

The Brigade keyed itself for battle. The old jokes came from the men, jests which had been repeated and repeated since the first skirmish. Red lines would be drawn through names in John Edwards' daily roster book before the sun had set and the men knew it—yet they joked.

The road curved down the rocky, jagged slopes toward the tree-lined river. The river was a rushing torrent and below the crossing could be heard the roar of a waterfall. The ambush site, if such a trap had been set, had been admirably chosen.

The column reached the outer shadows of the trees. Then came a short, sharp volley as Williams and his reconnoitering party received the first fire. He halted. His job was to uncover the ambush, not to attack. His trained ears and eyes told him the number of the guerrillas as if they had risen up from their positions and he had counted them. He withdrew a short distance and waited.

Elliott came on with his ten men, those who were to spearhead the charge and receive the first terrible broadside. Shelby had closed the distance to a hundred paces; before the battle had well begun the two bodies would become one.

Shelby galloped up to Williams.

"You found them, it seems."

"Yes, General."

"How many?"

"Eight hundred at the least."

"How armed?"

"With muskets."

"Good enough. Take your place in the front ranks. I shall lead the column."

He spoke to Elliott: "Advance instantly, Colonel. The sooner over the sooner to sleep. Take the water as you find it, and ride straight forward. Forward!"

Cundiff turned to Langhorne, who was riding at his right; "Have you said your prayers, Captain?"

"Too late now. Those who pray best pray first."

85

Elliott's advance party rode forward, first at a walk, then at a trot. He turned and shouted, "Keep your pistols dry. It will be hot work on the other side."

His party reached the river and slid down the rough, rocky banks. Shots rang out across the stream, scattering shots that soon became a steady volley.

The column thundered forward and rapidly closed the interval. Elliott reached the opposite bank and the firing grew desperate, though his party had not as yet fired a shot.

A wild yell, long and piercing, a yell that had exultation and death in it, broke from the Mexicans and Indians, and answering it came the blast of Martin Kritzer's bugle, and then the even-wilder Rebel Yell, which had struck fear to even steady and trained American troops in the war just past. The Brigade dashed into the river and splashed across.

Up ahead Elliott was lying under his dead horse badly wounded. Fell, shot through the hip, kept his seat and went on; Wood's left wrist was bloody so he pressed the bridle reins between his teeth and careened forward, firing his revolver with his right hand; Cundiff's left arm hung helpless and dripping red; McDougall and Winship and Langhorne were down. Only Rudd and Chiles and Kirtley and Woods were unscathed, and they grouped around their fallen comrades, steady and cool, not wasting a shot.

Shelby cleared the river, swept up the distant bank; the attack became a flaming hurricane of fire and sabre strokes. At intervals the bugle blast reverberated through the rocks and trees and underbrush, though no orders were needed. Wild Rebel yells told the story of the battle that became a massacre, for the Americans remembered the village and gave no quarter.

The Englishman's horse fell and he seized another. A mania of battle took possession of him. His sword rose and descended and with each falling came a gush of blood. A musket ball shattered his left leg from knee to ankle. He still pressed forward. Another musket ball struck him squarely in the chest and knocked him cleanly from the saddle. He smiled as rough hands lifted him and bore him back to the bank of the river.

Two hundred of the enemy fell in the brush and died there. The living threw away their weapons and fled in terror from

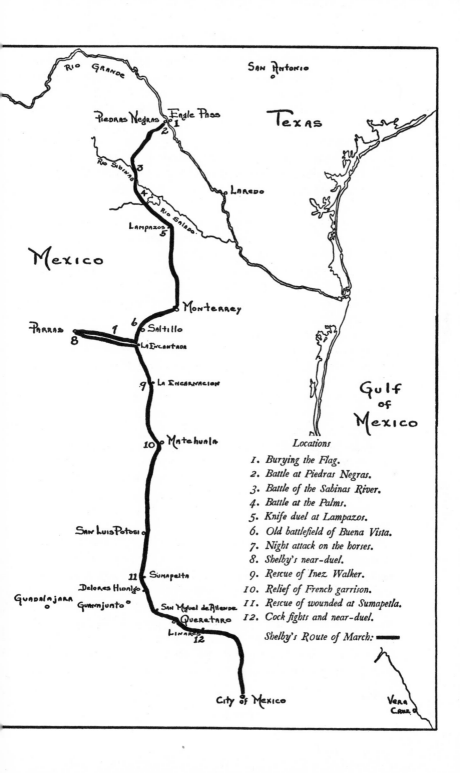

RIO GRANDE

SAN ANTONIO

TEXAS

Piedras Negras   Engle Pass 1
                            2

Rio Sibinas 3

4

LAREDO

Rio Salado

Lampazos
          5

Mexico

8 Monterrey

Parras   1   6   Saltillo
      8   La Encantada

9 La Encarnacion

10 Matehuala

San Luis Potosi

Gulf
of
Mexico

Locations

1. *Burying the Flag.*
2. *Battle at Piedras Negras.*
3. *Battle of the Sabinas River.*
4. *Battle at the Palms.*
5. *Knife duel at Lampazos.*
6. *Old battlefield of Buena Vista.*
7. *Night attack on the horses.*
8. *Shelby's near-duel.*
9. *Rescue of Inez Walker.*
10. *Relief of French garrison.*
11. *Rescue of wounded at Sumapetla.*
12. *Cock fights and near-duel.*

11 Sumapetla
Delores Hidalgo
Guadalajara   Guanajuato
             San Miguel de Allende
             Queretaro
Linares
      12

Shelby's Route of March: ▬▬▬

City of Mexico

Vera
Cruz

the planned ambush which had become a scene of horror. Many tried to escape by jumping into the river, but these were picked off or carried downstream and over the falls. Others tried to hide in the chaparral and mesquite but were ruthlessly hunted down and pistoled or sabred. Some tried to surrender but their piteous pleadings died gurgling in their throats. Not a prisoner had been taken and the butchery would grow in horror as its tale spread through Indian tepee and guerrilla *jacal* from the lower reaches of the Rio Bravo to the deserts of Chihuahua and Sonora.

But the victory had been dearly bought. Nineteen bodies were laid out on the river's bank and eight men had been lost in the river. Thirty-seven were wounded and several fatally.

The Englishman still lived. "Would you have a priest?" Shelby asked, as he leaned over him.

"None. No word nor prayer can avail me now. I shall die as I have lived."

Men who had just dealt death now turned sadly away from its presence.

"Who among you speaks French." The Englishman finally asked.

"Governor Reynolds."

"Send him to me, please."

Reynolds motioned the men away. The last words, the last explanation, the last confession, were to be for one man's ears alone. French would be spoken that none might understand. The story was later recounted to Sir James Scarlett, the British Minister in the City of Mexico, and afterwards to John Edwards.

The man was the youngest son of an English baron. He had entered the army as a young man and at twenty-two was a lieutenant in the Fourth Royals. While quartered in Ireland he had fallen in love with an Irish girl, but she had already given her heart to a young cornet in the same regiment and she tearfully rejected him. Insane with rage and jealousy the young lieutenant had pursued the cornet, insulted him, ridiculed him, and finally struck him. A challenge followed. The duel was fought and the cornet was killed; the lieutenant was tried, convicted and cashiered from the army. He became a wanderer, a soldier of fortune. For years he had recklessly courted death but for him death had taken a holiday. Death became an obsession and his mind had grown warped and wandering—hence the fixation for death in a railway carriage.

The dying man whispered on with his half-incoherent tale of a wasted life. "There is much blood upon my hands, and here and there a good deed that will atone a little, it may be, in the end." His comrades came over as he dropped back.

Then he roused and said, "It is so dreary to die in the night. One likes to have the sunlight for this." Governor Reynolds leaned over, then straightened. The man was dead.

The bodies were wrapped in blankets and graves were dug. The men of the Brigade stood silently while Shelby said a prayer. Then the volleys cracked out their last farewell and Martin Kritzer's bugle gave its clear, liquid notes to the night.

12. The Duel at Lampazos

THE BRIGADE remained in camp at the Sabinas River crossing for nearly a week, although the majority of the wounded were up and about in a few days, but still stiff and weak from loss of blood. The seriously wounded, however, had to be nursed back to health and Doctor John Tisdale was kept busy.

Meanwhile the routine of the armed camp continued—guards and pickets and daily drills. They had passed the first baptism of fire in Mexico, but Shelby realized that the further they proceeded into the country the more hazardous would be the journey; discipline and the old battle efficiency would be their only salvation. The men grumbled at long morning and afternoon drills but they, too, understood the necessity of them.

At last the wounded were able to be moved. They headed out on the march to Lampazos.

The pace was slow and toilsome for they had left the gently rolling flat lands and were gradually climbing into the foothills which ran down from the slopes of the Sierra Madre Oriental. Over to the northwest lay the Sierra de Santa Ana, westward was the Sierra Hermosa de Santa Rosa, and to the south rose the rough and jagged peaks of the Sierra de Oballos and the Sierras de Hermanas, the Sister Mountains. The broad slopes of the foothills were as devoid of vegetation as the plains they had just crossed and were latticed by dry, deep arroyos which slowed up the march.

Camps were now made with studied regard for defense; for outriding bands of guerrillas constantly ranged, out of gunshot but plainly in sight, along the flanks and at the rear. At night they tried to steal horses or sniped at men sitting around the campfires. On several occasions they made as if to charge, or tried to ride down pickets, or fired a sudden volley, but fled when a platoon moved out for a counterattack.

Constant vigilance was necessary and under its tension the men became irritable and sullen. They threatened reprisals against the people of the little villages through which they passed or even against the poor peons who tilled the tiny *milpas,* the fields and farms that were scattered throughout the hills. One night a raiding party was organized, but Shelby heard of it and the next morning ordered the men into line.

"There are some signs among you of bad discipline and I have called you out that you may be told of it." He explained their situation—an invading force in a hostile country, but in a country where the civilian population offered no resistance. The guerrilla bands must be constantly guarded against and would be fought at every opportunity, but the Brigade was an organized, disciplined army and would not molest civilians.

"He who robs, he who insults women, he who oppresses the unarmed and the aged, is an outcast to all the good fellowship of this command and shall be driven forth as an enemy to us all. Hereafter be as you have ever been, brave, true and honorable."

The threatened reprisals were forgotten.

As higher altitudes were reached the country became even more difficult. Shorter marches were necessary and bivouacs became less desirable. The air was thin and the cold more penetrating. The horses, unaccustomed to such conditions, weakened and many of them developed the inevitable fever. It was the rainy season of the year and the afternoon rains, piercing and cold, sometimes merged into night storms when the howling, freezing wind and the blowing rain made camp comfort impossible.

John Edwards later wrote of their plight: "Woe to the steed

who loses his blanket, and woe to the rider who sleeps while the cold night air is driving in death through every pore. Accordingly as the perspiration is checked or encouraged is the balance for or against the life of the horse." And Tisdale, a shaggy-headed, hearty-laughing, pipe-smoking man of fifty, was a tireless Good Samaritan to men and mounts when the cold night winds blew across the mountains of San Juan del Aguila and the frosts fell, and deep, exhausted sleep settled over the camp.

Finally the higher mountain passes were crossed and the Brigade moved more rapidly along the road to Lampazos. But guerrillas became more troublesome and the men begged to ride against them. "Let them alone," Shelby said, "and husband your strength. In a land of probable giants we have no need to hunt possible chimeras." He forbade pursuit of the small parties that at times rode almost to within gunshot distance.

One afternoon the expedition camped at a pass which crossed some low ridge spurs sloping down from the mountains. Between two of the ridges was a shallow, little valley through which tumbled a clear mountain stream lined with palm trees.

It was a peaceful, Eden-like place in the desert. Above them towered the palms, pensive, sadder voiced than pines, with no clinging vines and housing no nesting birds, and as Edwards said, "strange and shapely, and coldly chaste, they seem like human and desolate things, standing all alone in the midst of luxurious nature, unblessed of the soil, and unloved of the dew and sunshine." Underfoot the grass grew abundantly, so that the horses could be staked out close to camp.

The men went to sleep, except for the sentinels who silently walked their posts, the fires went out, and a low-hanging, white mist came up from the stream and settled over the camp.

Suddenly a pistol cracked off to the south, echoing clear and resonant in the night. Shelby raised himself on one elbow and said to John Thrailkill, the old Missouri-Kansas border fighter who never slept, and who had the senses of an Indian, "Who has the post at the mouth of the pass?"

"Joe Macey."

"Then something is stirring. Macey never fired at a shadow in his life."

91

The aroused camp listened for a while, but when there was no answering shot, promptly went back to sleep.

Suddenly from up the slopes of the ridge burst a solid sheet of flame. It was fired at close range, almost in the faces of the sleeping men, but the obscuring mists caused the raiders to fire too high; it swept over them and not a man was hit.

Shelby's voice rang out, "Give them the revolver. Charge!"

Although able to see nothing through the mists, the men charged, still groggy with sleep, half-clothed and shoeless but with a revolver in each hand and a Bowie knife at the belt. Up the slopes they went, firing at the ghostly spectres that appeared and then faded again into the white blanket that was the mist. Comrades were only recognized by their voices. The roars and old battle yells with which each had grown familiar through the years of fighting in the hills and valleys of Missouri and Arkansas again rang out along the line.

The Mexicans, who were led by a renegade priest named Juan Anselmo and Antonio Flores, a young Cuban who had come to Mexico and turned bandit, had halted on the other side of the mountain, tethered their horses, and, slipping past Macey and the other outposts, had crept upon the sleeping camp with all the stealth of the few Indians who had accompanied them and opened fire.

The battle was a furious hand-to-hand engagement but the charge was a hurricane, unstoppable and devastating. Tisdale and his detail gathered up the seventeen wounded men and brought in the bodies of eleven who had been killed. Seventy-one guerrilla bodies were left where they had fallen, including those of Anselmo and Flores, the leaders.

Again there was a ceremony at fresh mounds of earth, the prayer, the plaintive, sad calls of the bugle, and the rifle volley, which echoed along the palms that lined the banks of the little mountain stream. Then the Brigade moved out along the road to Lampazos.

Lampazos was an old town which had been founded during the fabulous years of the colonial era, when Spain was pushing her northern Mexican frontiers into what is now the United States. The town nestled in a deep, tree-filled valley. Behind it lay the blue crests of the Eastern Cordilleras while in front rose the almost perpendicular walls of the high Mesa de los Cartu-janos which had been the citadel of the powerful Cartujano In-dians during pre-Spanish days. Later the Benedictine Fathers had built a mission atop the hill, Christianized the natives and taught them agriculture and stock raising.

The town was an oversized pastoral village with the usual square, church, and checkerboard pattern of streets bordered by modest adobe and stucco, single-story houses. With the exception of a few *ricos* who lived in wall-surrounded mansions, the in-habitants were poor tradesmen, artisans and farmers.

Society was patriarchal in such towns of Old Mexico. Fathers governed their families with a stern hand, while priests and *alcaldes* laid down general regulations for religious and public conduct. The tempo of life was leisurely and was broken only by the celebration of births and marriages, solemn rites for the dead, and the enjoyment of the dozens of feast and *fiesta* days that thronged the year. Each feast or *fiesta* brought its *fandango* where young and old alike danced the old dances of Spain which had been modified through the years by Indians or *Mestizos*.

A grand *fandango* was in progress at Lampazos when the ex-pedition reached the town. Streamers hung across the streets, houses were decorated, and villagers and country people filled the little plaza. The entrance of another armed band caused little stir, for during the preceding half century Mexicans had become accustomed to armed bands; during recent years they had been either Juaristas or the followers of Emperor Maxi-milian. They shrugged their shoulders and went on with their dancing and merrymaking. The Brigade passed through the streets and went into camp just beyond the suburbs.

Guards were posted and the horses put to graze under heavy guard. Shelby ordered that no soldier was to leave camp, for marauding guerrillas were still about and he did not know the temper of the people of the village or their particular allegiance at the moment—were they followers of Juarez or had they cast their lot with the Empire?

But three men slipped out of camp and eluded the pickets. Wandering into town, they floated along with the flood tide of the *fandango,* drank at the *cantinas,* and danced with the brightly and quaintly dressed, attractive Indian or *mestizo* girls.

Late that night they started back to camp. Flushed with *mescal* and *tequila,* they walked carelessly along singing snatches of Bacchanal love songs of the Old Iron Brigade, laughing loudly, and waving or speaking to every passer-by.

Then a girl standing in an open doorway attracted them and Crockett accosted her. She spoke to him but the words were unintelligible. He made signs and she laughed at him. Finally he tried to kiss her and, alarmed by the suddenness of his movement, she screamed. Instantly there was a rush of men from the houses and the shadows of the street. The Americans were unarmed and in the melee Walker was shot through both cheeks and Boswell stabbed three times, though Crockett, who had caused the trouble, escaped without a wound.

No pursuit was attempted after the fight, and Boswell, who had not been seriously wounded, and Crockett helped Walker along the darkened streets toward camp. Soon, however, a Mexican drew up behind them in the shadows.

Crockett turned. "Why do you follow me?"

"That you may lead me to your General."

"What do you wish with my General?"

"Satisfaction."

Then the town patrol caught up with them, placed them under arrest, and, followed by a large crowd of Mexicans, carried them straight to Shelby. Shelby gave the two wounded men over to Tisdale, then turned to the officer of the patrol and the young man who had followed. The young man told the story of the fight and the incident which had led to it.

Pointing an accusing finger at Crockett, he said, "That man has outraged my sister. I could have killed him, but I did not. You Americans are brave, I know; will you be generous as well, and give me satisfaction."

Shelby looked at Crockett, but Crockett did not comprehend the meaning and implication of the Mexican's words.

"Does the Mexican speak truth, Crockett?"

"Partly, but I meant no harm to the woman. I am incapable of that. Drunk I know I was, and reckless, but not willfully guilty, General."

Shelby was stern. The order not to leave camp had been violated and he glared at the offender. "What business had you to

94

lay your hands upon her at all? How often must I repeat to you that the man who does these things is no follower of mine? Will you give her brother satisfaction?"

Dueling was a custom of Mexico as well as of the South. Crockett drew his revolver.

"No, not the pistol," said the Mexican. "I do not understand the pistol. The knife, *Señor* General, is the *Americano* afraid of the knife?"

Crockett nodded, "The knife, ah! Well, so be it. Will one of you give me a knife?"

A large circle was drawn on the ground. Under the Mexican custom of knife fighting neither combatant was to step from the ring. If he did so the witnesses were privileged to kill him, so the Mexicans, who now intermingled with the soldiers, drew knives and some of them pistols.

The two men stepped into the circle. Crockett looked at the knife which had been given him and checked its balance. The Mexican wound his *serape,* a lightweight, narrow blanket, around his left arm with which to ward off or catch the knife thrusts of his adversary (an old custom which ran back several hundred years to the days before the Spanish came to Mexico) and drew his own glittering, keen-edged blade.

Shelby turned. "Go for Tisdale," he said. "When the steel has finished the surgeon may begin."

The two men faced each other in the ring. The Mexican muttered a prayer and, with clenched hand, mechanically made the sign of the cross, his thumb extending toward his face (a ritual still practiced by Mexican athletes before a contest and bull fighters before facing the horns). Crockett remained motionless; he was accustomed to danger, had just passed through four years of war, and bore the scars of three wounds. He had faced fights to the death before. The Mexican bowed.

Crockett was the taller and stronger of the adversaries, but the Mexican had the look of agility and lightning speed. It would be an evenly matched fight.

The torches, only slightly stirred by the gentle breeze, flared in the night and assisted the rays of the moon. There was no sound, and the watching faces might have been cast in bronze, for not a man moved. Standing silently with emotionless eyes that

95

were used to death, Shelby gazed upon the strange scene—a scene which rolled back the ages to primitive men and knives of stone or copper, or to the Roman circus where slaves and Christians fought in the arena while maddened throngs yelled for the final thrust for him who was on his knees.

The two men advanced upon each other and began to circle.

The Mexican suddenly attacked. Lowering his head and with his arm held up so that only his face could be seen, he charged at Crockett. His right arm thrust at Crockett's breast. Crockett threw up his left arm as a shield and the Mexican's blade buried itself in his shoulder. Then he moved quickly to the right and as his adversary half turned to follow the movement, struck home, sinking his knife to the hilt in the Mexican's breast.

The night was cool and for the Mexican there would be no bright sunshine of morning. He dropped lifeless on the ground, the knife sticking up grotesquely under the flickering light of the torches.

Friends lifted his bloody body and bore it back to Lampazos, where throughout the night a grief-stricken mother rocked slowly back and forth listening to the cries of a sweetheart iterating and reiterating the legacy of her grief.

V

MONTERREY
TO PARRAS

13. Monterrey

MONTERREY HAD LIVED A vacillating and irresolute existence during the Mexican reform years of the 1850's; its conduct had been no more steadfast since the coming of Maximilian to Mexico. The *ciudadanos* sided first with Juarez, then with the Emperor. When the armies of Juarez were in the vicinity they declared enthusiastically for the Liberals; when Juarez was forced to retire they yelled just as loudly for Maximilian and Carlota.

During the previous ten years Governor Santiago Vidaurri had governed the states of Coahuila and Nuevo Leon as if he had been king over an independent domain. He was the *cacique,* the chief, and the dictator of the entire northeastern frontier. Attached to his seigniory with all the pride of a more paternal despot, extremely popular with the people through his ostentatious maneuverings, highly jealous of his rank, title and authority, he played a deep game of political neutrality with both Juarez and the Emperor.

Former President Ignacio Comonfort of Mexico had once exclaimed: "Vidaurri must be attracted or eliminated. I favor the former extreme." Juarez was also hopeful that he could be steadfastly attached to the Liberal cause, but Vidaurri finally sided with the Emperor and upon the approach of the Liberal army escaped to the United States.

In late 1864 Juarez controlled most of northern Mexico, so the people of Monterrey shouted and made *fiestas.* Six months later Nuevo Leon and Tamaulipas were in the hands of the Empire—and they shouted and made *fiestas.* Then Juarez returned and the populace again shouted and made *fiestas,* while Juarez confidently planned for the eventual success of his cause:

97

"Soon the fire will assume colossal forms, and we shall see whether Maximilian is capable of smothering it."

In early July, 1865, just as Shelby was entering the country, the Empire forces launched an offensive against Northern Mexico. Juarez lost Monterrey and the people of the town shouted and made *fiestas* in honor of Colonel Pierre Jean Joseph Jeanningros, the French officer who had been appointed military governor of the Monterrey district. Juarez retreated to El Paso. Jeanningros stationed garrisons at Saltillo, about fifty miles southwest of Monterrey, and at Parras, some seventy-five miles west of Saltillo, but the rest of northeastern Mexico was in a state of complete anarchy and armed bands crisscrossed the land plundering and killing either in the name of Mexican liberty or in the name of the Emperor.

This was the situation, then, as Shelby led his men southward from Piedras Negras toward the City of the Saddle. Juarez had temporarily been beaten back. In the City of Mexico the Emperor and Empress were confident of victory and of establishing their empire and had begun Mexicanizing themselves. "We dress *a la Mexicaine,*" Carlota wrote the French Empress Eugenie, "I wear a sombrero when riding. We eat *a la Mexicaine,* we have a carriage with many mules and bells, we are always wrapped in serapes, I go to Mass in a mantilla." Carlota only partially wrote the truth—there is no evidence, except her own statement, that she or Maximilian were quite so enthusiastic about things Mexican.

The decision of Shelby's men to join the Emperor had been made at the Rio Grande. Since leaving Piedras Negras, however, Shelby had received word that Jeanningros had been furious that he had sold the Liberals his supplies, guns and artillery and had sworn to punish him: "Let me but get my hands upon these Americans," he had said, "these *canaille,* and after that we can see."

Shelby had decided, however, to continue the march to Monterrey and if the French officer was still stubborn and vindictive either to attack him or return to Piedras Negras, recruit a large force of ex-Confederates and then move against the capital of Nuevo Leon. In order to secure information as to the French commandant's intentions, as well as his strength, he sent young

Rainy McKinney ahead from Lampazos to Monterrey. Perhaps the opportunity would be found to secure the desired information.

McKinney found the town filled with ex-Confederates. Several state governors were there, including Moore and Allen of Louisiana. Generals Walker, Smith and Preston were awaiting the opportunity to go to some gulf port and book passage to Cuba; Wilcox, Magruder, Price, and Hindman were stopping over briefly before pushing on to the City of Mexico. A few ex-Confederates had already joined the Emperor's forces and had been sent to garrisons in the interior of the country.

A squadron of about a hundred men captained by Frank Moore of Alabama had joined the Contre-Guerrillas, a newly-organized regiment under the command of a French soldier of fortune, Colonel François Achille Dupin.

Dupin had become known as "The Tiger of the Tropics," for he was a bloodthirsty old devil who regarded brutality and murder as a fine art. He had soldiered all over the world with the French army and, after having led in the looting and sacking of the Emperor's palace in China, had been court martialed. He had conducted his own defense and had parodied the famous speech of Warren Hastings: "When I saw mountains of gold and precious stones piled up around me, and when I think of the paltry handfuls taken away, by G-d, Mr. President, I am astonished at my own moderation."

After he had been convicted, cashiered out of the army and stripped of his decorations and honors, he drew himself up with an air of dignity, saluted the court, and said: "They have left me nothing but my scars."

Eventually, however, Louis Napoleon had need of him in Mexico, so he was given back his rank and his decorations. But Maximilian refused to receive him, so he was sent north to organize the regiment of Contre-Guerrillas.

Dupin was past sixty years of age but still sat his saddle like an English guardsman. He was tall and lithe and his snow-white hair and beard contrasted with the bronzed, nut-brown face which had been darkened by the sun and wind and rain of fifty strenuous campaigns. His countenance was set and hard; it was said that he only smiled when in battle.

He had a theory about Juarista Liberals, a diabolical theory which he put into practice as often as possible: "When you kill a Mexican that is the end of him. When you cut off an arm or a leg, that throws him upon the charity of his friends, and then two or three must support him. Those who make corn can not make soldiers. It is economy to amputate."

His maimed and mutilated lived in every town in northern Mexico, for hundreds had passed through the hands of his surgeons. When the march had been pleasant or his battle plans completely successful or he felt playful, he permitted chloroform or wine, otherwise not. But it distressed him to see one of his victims die under the knife: "You bunglers endanger my theory. Why can't you cut without killing?"

Perhaps Dupin's most treacherous deed had been the hanging of the wealthy Mexican hacendado, Don Vicente Ibarra. Ibarra had been Liberal in sympathy, yet he had not taken up arms or aided Juarez, and he had paid the taxes levied by Jeanningros without a murmur of protest. Dupin had Ibarra brought to his camp where he greeted him with all evidences of friendship: "Be seated," he said pleasantly, "And, waiter, lay another plate for my friend."

Ibarra was suspicious but Dupin plied him with compliments and wine; it was a delightful meal. Cigars and more wines were brought. Suddenly, Dupin's face darkened. He pointed to a large tree which stood just outside the tent. "What a fine shade it makes, *Señor*. Do such trees ever bear fruit?"

No, such trees never bore fruit.

"Never? All things are possible with God, why not with a Frenchman?"

Dupin's darkened face grew still more cloudy.

"Are your affairs prosperous, *Señor?*"

"As much so as these times will permit."

"Very good. You have just five minutes in which to make them better. At the end of that time I will hang you on that tree so sure as you are a Mexican." And Ibarra was hanged. The tree had borne fruit.

One day word was brought Dupin that General Mosby M. Parsons of Missouri and five members of his party had been killed at Camargo, a small village on the Rio Grande, by guer-

Dupin's Contre-Guerrillas, from an old print.

rillas. They had attempted to overtake Shelby on his march from San Antonio to Piedras Negras, but missing him, had crossed the Rio Grande lower down the river, and had been ambushed, captured and then murdered. Dupin called his officers together. He asked Captain Frank Moore abruptly: "What would you Americans have?"

"Permission to gather up what is left of our comrades and bury what is left."

"And strike a good, fair blow in return?"

"Maybe so, Colonel."

"Then march at daylight with your squadron. Let me hear when you return that not one stone upon another of the robber's rendezvous has been left."

Moore caught them at the little village of Las Flores, swept into town, and began a massacre. He lost fifteen men but wiped out the bandits and left Las Flores not a city of flowers but a city of the dead. His former ex-Confederate comrades had been avenged.

Dupin, when Moore returned, shouted: "Oh! brave Ameri-

101

cans. Americans after my own heart. You shall be saluted with sloping standards and uncovered heads." He ordered a dress parade and the American squadron passed in review before lowered flags and uncovered lines of the Contre-Guerrillas.

When McKinney rejoined Shelby a day's march from Monterrey he brought word of these and other events which had recently occurred in the district held by Colonel Jeanningros. He also brought word that, while Jeanningros had somewhat softened in his threats against Shelby, he had not completely forgiven him for the sale of the supplies, guns and artillery to the Juarista forces, and that when Jeanningros had be n told of Shelby's advance and his officers had urged an attack he had said: "Wait awhile. We must catch them before we hang them."

Shelby, therefore, was faced with a dilemma. He could march boldly up to the gates of Monterrey, call Jeanningros' hand and hope for the best, or he could return to Piedras Negras to recruit a larger force. He did not hesitate. He ordered the march to continue.

It was late in July when Shelby drew up his men in long battle front only four miles outside Monterrey. He had less than a thousand men, while McKinney had reported that Jeanningros commanded a force of over five thousand and that the wall against which he shot his prisoners was never free of undried blood.

Shelby decided upon a swift, fearless and bold course of action. He called Governor Reynolds and ordered him to write a communication to Jeanningros. When it was finished he called for McKinney and Thrailkill and gave them the message.

Under a flag of truce the two men rode toward the city, galloped up to the pickets, and were given safe conduct to Jeanningros. Meanwhile, Shelby moved up to within a mile of the French defenses.

The French bugles blew and the long roll called the soldiers to arms while orderlies galloped through the streets. Jeanningros would receive the emissaries of the ex-Confederate general who had so boldly ridden up to within easy cannon shot of his lines.

McKinney and Thrailkill were brought in. Jeanningros had been attracted by the soldierly boldness of the action. His face softened a little as he read the message. Then he smiled. Here was a general after his own heart. He said to the two couriers: "Tell your general to march in immediately. He is the only soldier that has yet come out of Yankeedom."

Shelby's communication had read:

General:

I have the honor to report that I am within one mile of your fortifications with my command. Preferring exile to surrender, I have left my own country to seek service in that held by His Imperial Majesty, the Emperor Maximilian. Shall it be peace or war between us? If the former, and with your permission, I shall enter your lines at once, claiming at your hands that courtesy due from one soldier to another. If the latter, I propose to attack you immediately.

Very respectfully,
Yours,
J. O. Shelby.

14. Colonel Jeanningros

THRAILKILL AND McKinney smartly saluted the French commander, about-faced and marched out of his headquarters. They went down the stairs and out the arched entrance of the Palacio Municipal, a building which had been built during the 1850's in the usual architectural style of Mexican public buildings, with portales, supported by massive pillars, running around the entire structure. The portales were large enough to shelter a regiment, though no more than a company of soldiers lounged about, but in the Plaza de Zaragoza in front of the building several companies were drawn up in readiness for action.

Mounting their horses, the two men followed their escort along Zaragoza, Morelos, Juarez streets, passed the market and the Alameda, and arrived at the northern edge of town. They found the Brigade drawn up in battle formation and reported to Shelby.

Shelby was pleased at the favorable turn of events and ordered the Brigade forward into the city. Jeanningros, who had assigned quarters by the time it had reached the Palacio Municipal, received Shelby with friendly, old world courtesy, con-

103

gratulated him upon his boldness and soldierly manner of action, and invited him to a banquet that evening.

Many ex-Confederate civil and military officials were present, among them Governor Reynolds, Senators Trusten Polk of Missouri and William M. Gwin of California, and Generals John B. Magruder, Thomas C. Hindman, John B. Clark, and Kirby Smith. The dinner was lavish and Jeanningros a superb host. Wine loosened his tongue and he reminisced with all the facility of a raconteur—campaigns in the Crimea, in Italy, in Algeria, the march to Peking, Napoleon III's *coup d'etat,* great soldiers he had known, and personal adventures that extended over twenty years of army life. His knowledge of the American Civil War which had just ended was broad and extensive and he left no doubt that his sympathies had been with the South. He discussed the possible effects of the war's ending upon the diplomatic relations between the United States and France and upon the empire of Maximilian. He was friendly and frank— and Shelby was impressed.

Shelby finally asked him about the diplomatic abilities of Maximilian.

"Ah! the Austrian; you should see him to understand him. More of a scholar than a king, good at botany, a poet on occasions, a traveler who gathers curiosities and writes books, a saint over his wine and a sinner among his cigars, in love with his wife, believing more in manifest destiny than drilled battalions, good Spaniard in all but deceit and treachery, honest, earnest, tender-hearted and sincere, his faith is too strong in the liars who surround him, and his soul is too pure for the deeds that must be done."

His analysis of Maximilian had so far been accurate.

"He can not kill as we Frenchmen do. He knows nothing of diplomacy. In a nation of thieves and cut-throats, he goes devoutly to mass, endows hospitals, laughs a good man's laugh at the praises of the blanketed rabble, says his prayers and sleeps the sleep of the gentleman and the prince."

Jeanningros warmed to his subject. He continued: "Bah! his days are numbered; nor can all the power of France keep his crown upon his head, if, indeed, it can keep that head upon his shoulders."

104

Then Jeanningros suddenly checked himself. He had gone too far. He had spoken too frankly. He was a soldier, not a diplomat, and an officer of the French Army should not have permitted a little wine at a dinner to have so loosened his tongue.

General Clark spoke up. "Has he the confidence of Bazaine?"

Jeanningros paused, lifted the goblet and drained it, and shrugged. "The Marshal, you mean. Oh! the Marshal keeps his own secrets. Besides I have not seen the Marshal since coming northward. Do you go further, General Clark?"

Jeanningros was again himself. His natural French suavity and diplomacy had returned. Both men smiled. There would be no more frank outpourings of the mind. Light chat and the personalities of those present would occupy them until the banquet's end.

It was almost daylight when the Americans returned to their quarters. Jeanningros, however, had an official duty to perform. A court-martial had met that night. A man had been convicted. He must sign a death warrant.

One of the Foreign Legion's young lieutenants had drunk too much wine and had abandoned his post, and for three days had been missing. When he finally recovered his senses, he realized what he had done. Two courses of action lay open to him. He could either desert, flee northward and cross the Rio Grande, or he could return to his post and face a court-martial. The first course would permit him life but would bring disgrace to himself and to his family; the second would bring conviction and death before a firing squad, and disgrace. In either case, disgrace could not be avoided. He did not hesitate, but returned to his post and surrendered. His court-marital and conviction was but a matter of routine.

Late that night he wrote Jeanningros a note. He begged for the opportunity of suicide. This way his property would go to his mother, rather than to the state. And he closed his communication: "It is a little thing a soldier asks of his General, who has medals, and honors, and, maybe a mother, too—but for the sake of the uniform I wore at Solferino, is it asking more than you can grant when I ask for a revolver and a bottle of brandy?"

Jeanningros read the note and called an aide. "Take to the commandant of the prison this order." The order read that a

bottle of good brandy and a revolver be delivered to the lieutenant's cell immediately.

The next morning when the guards unlocked the cell they
found an empty brandy bottle and the body of the dead lieutenant. Jeanningros smiled when the news was brought to him,
"Clever fellow. He was entitled to two bottles instead of one."

The French Army never permitted the military crime of desertion to go unpunished; its inexorable justice had been carried
out. Jeanningros' long years of military service had made him
a hardened, callous commander, but even in a day of strict and
severe discipline his discipline was unusually severe. Occasionally, however, he could show slight evidences of mercy and com-
passion. The Americans would be impressed. He was well satisfied with himself.

It was Shelby's purpose to take service with the Mexican
Empire of Maximilian of Austria. His men had so voted at Eagle
Pass when they had refused to become the followers of Benito
Juarez and his Liberal party. He must gain the cooperation of
Colonel Jeanningros, for Jeanningros would make recommenda-
tions in his communications to Marshal Bazaine in the City of
Mexico.

Jeanningros was a soldier and would understand a soldier's
arguments. The long years in camp and barracks and the hard
campaigns had made him cruel, it was true, but he would
listen to the logic of military necessity. The gray-haired officer,
who bore the scars of thirteen battle wounds and who was still
able to hold his own in a bout over a bottle of absinthe, would
listen to Shelby's plans for enlisting a corps of Americans to de-
fend Maximilian's throne.

For the next several days Jeanningros and Shelby discussed
plans and argued strategy. Shelby used all the wily diplomatics
he could muster and one can imagine that John Edwards was
a strong ally at these meetings with the French commandant.

Shelby proposed that he be granted the use of a seaport as
a base of operations from which to collect supplies and concentrate the thousands of enlistees from the South and the North
who would soon pour into Mexico. A port on the Gulf of Mexico
would not serve as advantageously as would a port on the Gulf
of Lower California or the Pacific, for the French already held

the entire eastern portion of Mexico, while the western, north-western and central western sections of the Empire made up the great stronghold of Juarez. Shelby preferred either Guaymas, which was on the Gulf of Lower California in Sonora about four hundred and fifty miles southwest of Chihuahua, or Mazatlan, a Pacific port in Sinaloa about three hundred and seventy-five miles northwest of Guadalajara. The American legion would be mobilized at one of these points and from this base of operations would begin action against the Liberals.

During the period of these conferences with Jeanningros, Shelby relied heavily on the advice of William M. Gwin, for Gwin was a brilliant and experienced statesman and knew the Mexican diplomatic situation as few knew it. After having represented Mississippi in Congress, he had gone to California, which he had served with John C. Fremont in the United States Senate. Imprisoned during the first two years of the war, he had been released and had gone to France where he had had an audience with Maximilian, who gave his approval of a vast colonization scheme in Sonora. He went to Mexico to implement the scheme, but Bazaine gave him no encouragement and the Emperor changed his mind, so he returned to France in January, 1865, and frankly disclosed the true situation in Mexico to Napoleon III. Napoleon sent him again to Mexico with orders to Bazaine to supply the necessary troops fully to accomplish the colonization plan. But Bazaine seemed amused at his ideas for a great dukedom in the northwest, and the Emperor had become disgusted. Gwin was now on his way to Matamoras to leave Mexico.

Next to Gwin, Shelby drew most heavily upon the advice of General John B. Clark of Missouri. Clark was a gallant officer and still limped from the wound he had received at Wilson's Creek. During the march from San Antonio, his nightly camp-fire tales, anecdotes and reminiscences had been a great stimulus to morale, but he had also caused Shelby considerable trouble, for he constantly pled for active service with the Brigade. At the Battle of the Sabinas River he had ridden up to Shelby, armed and ready for a fight.

"Where would you go?" asked Shelby.

"As far as you go, my young man."

"Not this day, my old friend, if I can help it. There are younger and less valuable men who shall take this risk alone. Get out of the ranks, General. The column can not advance unless you do."

And General Clark had sworn his rough Anglo-Saxon oaths and had been mad for a week, only completely recovering his usual amiability when he had been permitted (Shelby could not have prevented it anyhow) to fight in the night attack at the Pass of the Palms.

While these conferences and discussions were going on Shelby's men took the welcome opportunity to enjoy the pleasures of Monterrey; after all, it was the largest city they had seen since leaving San Antonio. They wandered through the walks of the plazas and visited the old cathedral (which had been used as a powder magazine and which had been badly damaged during the American Invasion), where they saw the little image of the Virgin of Roble which had been found by an Indian in an oak log back in the sixteenth century. They wandered out to the Bishop's Palace atop Chepe Vera Hill, the hill that had been captured by the Americans only after a hotly-contested fight. They went to the hot springs of Topo Chico, only a few miles northwest of the city, and took the baths—had not a daughter of the Aztec emperor Moctezuma been miraculously cured there shortly before Cortez's conquest of the Aztec Empire? They visited the Garcia Caves and Huasteca Canyon, climbed to the top of Chipinque Mesa behind the town, and saw the great cataract tumbling over the cliff at Horsetail Falls, a couple of miles west of the little village of El Cerdado.

At night they joined the young unmarried men and women of the town at the Plaza Zaragoza and participated with them in the old custom of circling the square in opposite directions until couples formed, who then promenaded to the melodious music of the military band under the watchful eyes of the *duenas*. And some of the knights errant successfully melted the hearts of the *señoritas,* were taken over to the benches where they were introduced, and were permitted to talk a while.

They visited the *cantinas* where they drank *mescal* and *tequila,* the fiery-hot, national drinks of the country, or the cafes where they ate roast young goat, grilled beef ribs, beans with

108

chicharron, and dry beef gravy—all distinctive dishes of the town.

The majority of the men hoped that the conferences and dinners of their chief would never end, though some of them chafed at the delay and left the Brigade, to go to Sonora to join Liberal General Antonio Corona, to California, to British Honduras, to Brazil, or to enlist in the American company under Colonel Dupin.

At last the conferences ended. The Brigade would move to Mazatlan, by way of Saltillo, past the old Mexican War battle-field of Buena Vista, Parras and the Laguna country, Gomez Palacio, and Durango.

Shelby had his last meeting with Jeanningros. He re-emphasized the present diplomatic position of the United States. France and Maximilian should have made an alliance with the South long ago: "Better battles could have been fought on the Potomac than on the Rio Grande; surer results would have followed from a French landing at Mobile than at Tampico or Vera Cruz. You have waited too long."

Jeanningros waited.

"Flushed with a triumphant termination of the war, American diplomacy now means the Monroe doctrine, pure and simple, with a little Yankee brutality and braggadocio thrown in."

Jeanningros agreed and heard him to the end, then answered frankly that there would be no war between France and the United States. There was no love lost between the Emperor of Mexico and Bazaine, for one was a scholar and the other a soldier. He admitted that he did not know the intentions of Bazaine regarding the ex-Confederates, but did not believe that Bazaine would refuse their offers of assistance.

"You have my full permission to march to the Pacific, and to take such other steps as will seem best to you in the matter of which you have just spoken. The day is not far distant when every French soldier in Mexico will be withdrawn, although this would not necessarily destroy the Empire. Who will take their places?"

Shelby waited.

"Mexicans. Bah! beggars ruling over beggars, cut-throats lying in wait for cut-throats, traitors on the inside making signs for

109

traitors on the outside to come in. Not thus are governments upheld and administered. Healthy blood must be poured through every effete and corrupted vein of this effete and corrupted nation ere the Austrian can sleep a good man's sleep in his palace of Chapultepec."

The two men shook hands and Shelby rode off to join his men. The Brigade formed and, with the guidon flying proudly at the front of the column, headed out on the road to Saltillo.

15. The Road to Parras

SKIRTING THE old Mexican War forts Diable and Teneria, the Brigade moved out past the Campo Santo Cemetery and the *Obispado* (Bishop's Palace) on the Saltillo road. The old *camino* gradually ascended until the village of Santa Caterina was reached, then it dipped and passed through large groves of trees and maguey until it arrived at the ravaged hacienda of Rinconada, which lay in a green valley, traversed by running streams. Here the majestic ranges of the Sierra Madre Oriental closed in and the road, turning sharply to the left, plunged upward through the grand and sombre gorge of Rinconada Pass. Some distance beyond the summit it passed the village of Milpas de los Muertos and into the broad valley which continued on to Saltillo.

The semitropical climate of Monterrey with its groves of orange and lemon trees slowly changed as the altitude grew higher; at Saltillo it was comparable to that of New England and here the men saw fields of oats and wheat and orchards of apples and cherries. During the first day the men had been marked with the cavalry war paint of dust and perspiration; by the time they made their second camp the night air was thin and cold.

Anything could be expected here and the daily drills were renewed; the old familiar commands rang out—"Dismount"—"Horse holders take the mounts"—"Troop attention"—"Prepare to fight on foot"—"At intervals, take distance. March." And the men grumbled as they always grumbled, but they realized the necessity of constant drill and of always being ready for an attack, even though the country had been "pacified" by the French.

110

Pass of Rinconada, southwest of Monterrey.

Near sunset the first evening out of Saltillo the command camped near the Mexican War battlefield of Buena Vista (called La Angostura by the Mexicans from the hacienda of the same name) which lay between two high mountain ridges about five miles south of the town. Some of the soldiers recalled incidents and tales of the Mexican War days—how Zachary Taylor's colored bodyservant had always referred to him as "de ole hoss," how Europeans had said that the Mexicans would "tear from the invader's flag the symbol of Texas," and how, after Taylor's success at Monterrey, Americans recited or hummed the stanza

Old Zack's at Monterrey
Bring out your Santa Anner;
For every time we raise a gun,
Down goes a Mexicanner.

General Thomas C. Hindman, who had been a soldier in Colonel Jefferson Davis' regiment, explored the battlefield with some of the men and regaled them with battle incidents:

111

Here Dr. Pedro Vanderlinden, Santa Anna's chief medical officer, had met General Taylor on February 22, 1847, the day before the battle, and had informed him that he was surrounded by 20,000 Mexicans and should surrender before he was cut to pieces. Here the band had played "Hail Columbia" and the men had used "Honor of Washington" as the password. Here General Taylor had spent the bitterly-cold and rainy night, huddled on the ground without a fire, as had the entire army.

Over there had been the Mexican camp and, in front of it, on the morning of the 23rd, the Mexican army had been lined up to hear Mass and a band concert of sacred music. Silken flags and banners and guidons flew from their staffs in front of the units. The soldiers, dressed in all the rainbow's colors, stood stiffly at attention. The officers, wearing their brightly-colored plumes, strutted about. Just before the battle, Santa Anna had ridden along the line, while tremendous *"vivas"* rolled down from the mountains with mighty echoes.

Here had been the American left flank; there black-eyed Hardin had died and there the gallant McKee had fallen, and there young Henry Clay, the son of the great statesman, the immortal Mill Boy of The Slashes. Over there, far in advance of his men, the lance point had found Yell's dauntless heart. There, along the crest of the hill, the Mississippians had formed, and there, in support, had been Bragg's Battery.

Here, yes, this was the place where Taylor, mounted on "Old Whitey," had said to Bragg, "Double-shot your guns and give 'em Hell!" And over there, when he saw McKee's regiment stagger, he had cried, as if the men could hear him, "By G-d, this will not do; this is not the way for Kentuckians to behave." And here he had been when McKee's men had rallied, where he had raised up in his stirrups and had shouted: "Hurrah for Old Kentuck! That's the way to do it. Give 'em Hell, damn 'em!"

And perhaps the general recalled how Santa Anna was reported to have said after the battle: "We whipped the Americans half a dozen times, and once completely surrounded them; but they would not stay whipped."

John Edwards well described that night, as the men of the Brigade sat around their fires and lived through another day, not twenty years past, in the history of their old country: "The battle-field lay under the great, calm face of the sky—a sepulchre. Looking out from his bivouac who knows what visions came to the musing soldier, as grave after grave gave up its dead, and as spirit after spirit put on its uniform and its martial array. Pale squadrons galloped again through the gloom of the powder-pall; again the deep roar of the artillery lent its mighty voice to swell the thunder of the gathering battle; again the rival flags rose and fell in the 'hot, lit foreground of the fight'; again the Lancers charge; piercing and sweet and wildly shrill, the bugles again called out for victory."

Finally the men lay down to sleep and the fires went out. The moon set over the mountains and the mirage faded into the shadows. The guards walked their posts and the mounted pickets circled the camp. It was only a long-ago-fought-battlefield lying under the stars, quiet save for the occasional rustle of the leaves in the trees, the low calls of birds and the gentle gusts of the night wind. The next morning the Brigade moved south to La Encantada and turned westward toward Parras.

Two nights before reaching Parras a terrific rainstorm inun-dated the camp, put out the fires and made sleep impossible. Dick Collins, James Kirtley, James Meadow and George Winship were stationed on picket duty at the mouth of a small mountain valley on the northern side of the line of march. Suddenly through the beating rain they saw dark shapes take form against the skyline and they drew cautiously behind the rocks which had been tossed down from the heights.

Winship said to Collins: "There is game afoot. No peaceful thing travels on such a devil's night as this."

The four men drew closer together and checked their rifles. There was a sudden volley from the guerrillas and they ad-vanced slowly over the uneven ground. The pickets fired at the gun flashes and held their position; soon the Mexicans closed in on them with revolver and knife. Kirtley was wounded in the left arm; Collins was bleeding at the right shoulder; Meadow and Winship were only slightly wounded. Still the four held their ground.

Then came the notes of the bugle and the rush of re-inforcements to the rescue. They swept past the pickets and engaged the guerrillas at close quarters. The sounds of the wind and the rain intermingled with the din of shots and yelling men. The marauders slowly gave ground, drawing Shelby further away from camp.

All at once a furious volley of shots was heard in the rear. The horses! The attack on the pickets had been but a feint to draw the main body of the men away from the horses. The real attack was to the rear, where Slayback and Cundiff with ten men guarded the staked-out horses.

Shelby yelled: "Countermarch for your lives. Make haste!—make haste!—the very clouds are raining Mexicans to-night."

The men turned and rushed the quarter-mile distance back to the horse lot where Slayback and Cundiff were desperately fighting. They could not afford to lose their mounts; horses were a matter of life or death in this country. Guards and pickets and some of the men still in camp rushed to the relief of Slayback and Cundiff.

It was a short hand-to-hand conflict, during which the men charged furiously against their adversaries who, because of the rain and the storm, were hard to distinguish from their comrades, but was the most furious battle of the entire expedition, for the guerrillas had attacked at two points with unusual ferocity. Dozens of Mexicans had been killed and wounded, but the price of victory had been heavy. The next morning there were graves to be dug, a prayer to be said, a volley fired, followed by the soft, mournful notes of a bugle.

Several parties of ex-Confederates awaited Shelby's arrival in Parras, for they had heard that he had been given permission by Colonel Jeanningros to proceed to Mazatlan and they proposed to join the expedition. In addition to a detachment of about twenty-five Texans, there were several smaller groups, one led by Colonel David S. Terry, former Chief Justice of the Supreme Court of California.

Upon Shelby's arrival, he was informed by the Americans that Colonel Marguerite Jacques Vincent du Preuil, who was the commandant of the garrison, had received an official communication from Marshal Bazaine specifically concerning his expedition. Bazaine had informed Preuil that Shelby's force was the beginning of an invasion of Mexico by Americans who intended undoubtedly to overrun the whole country completely, side with Juarez and the Liberals, and make war upon both the French and the Emperor. Shelby was therefore to be stopped at Parras and turned back toward the United States; if he refused to return north of the Rio Grande, he was to proceed without delay to the City of Mexico.

Shelby immediately sought an audience with Colonel Preuil. Preuil was the commanding officer of the 12th Regiment of Chasseurs, called "Cazadores a Caballo" in the imperial dispatches of Maximilian, light cavalry. Only a short time before, on the sixth of July, he had been honored by the Emperor who had elevated him to the rank of "Comendador", knight commander, of the Order of Guadalupe. He was impulsive, short-tempered, and sometimes overbearing; that he had other and more commendable qualities was subsequently to be proven to General Shelby.

Preuil lounged at his desk, ill-tempered, abusive and half drunk. He would make short shift of these Americans. Shelby was shown in. He removed his hat and advanced toward the Colonel with outstretched hand. The French officer only glared at him. Uninvited, Shelby turned and found the nearest chair. The two men studied each other.

"I have called, Colonel," said Shelby, "for permission to continue my march to Sonora."

"Such permission is impossible."

Shelby waited.

"You will turn aside to Mexico."

Shelby was astounded. He had frankly and completely discussed plans with Jeanningros, who had given him permission to proceed either to Guaymas or to Mazatlan. Had Preuil really received orders from Bazaine to turn him southward to the City of Mexico or was the Colonel personally responsible for the decision?

"May I ask the reason of this sudden resolution?"

Colonel Preuil only looked at him.

"Colonel Jeanningros had no information to this effect when I left him the other day in Monterrey."

Preuil rose in sudden fury at the mention of Jeanningros' name. Was this Yankee upstart trying to threaten him with the authority of his superior? He swayed drunkenly and shouted in Shelby's face: "What do I care for your information? Let the devil fly away with you and your information. It is the same old game you Americans are forever trying to play—robbing to-day and killing to-morrow—and plundering, plundering, plundering all the time."

Preuil paused for want of breath, while storm clouds gathered on Shelby's face. "You shall not go to Sonora, and you shall not stay here; but whatever you do you shall obey."

Shelby slowly rose, put on his hat, and advanced toward Preuil. Preuil's aide moved over against the wall. The guards followed him. They had seen their Colonel in anger before, had seen him browbeat men, but here was a man who obviously was not accustomed to being browbeaten. Trouble was imminent.

Shelby stopped a couple of paces in front of the French Colonel. His face and the unnatural huskiness of his voice revealed the intensity of his anger.

"I am mistaken it seems. I imagined that when an American soldier called upon a French soldier, he was at least visiting a gentleman."

He paused in order that the half-drunken man might comprehend the studied insult. Then he continued: "One can not always keep his hands clean, and I wash mine of you because you are a slanderer and a coward."

The insult had been deliberately given. It was now Preuil's turn.

Preuil laid his hand upon the hilt of his sword and made a motion as if to withdraw it. Shelby's right hand went to his holster, unbottoned the flap, and grasped the handle of the revolver. His officers drew closer.

With an insulting gesture, Preuil pointed to Shelby's hat and yelled: "Remove that."

Shelby's anger was now gone. His voice was cutting and cold, sarcastic, but it was calm, a terrible calmness that hinted of death.

"To a coward, never," he said. He had twice called Colonel Preuil a coward.

Preuil glanced at his guard, then at the silent figures of the Americans. He looked back at Shelby and grasped the hilt of his sword, but the motion died there.

Then with an oath, he screamed, "Retire—retire instantly—lest I outrage all hospitality and dishonor you in my own house. You shall pay for this—you shall apologize for this."

Without another word, Shelby turned and walked from the room.

Shelby returned to his quarters just outside the town and sent for Governor Reynolds. The two men were closeted for an hour. Then Reynolds rode off in the direction of the square and Colonel Preuil's headquarters.

Preuil, who had sobered in the meantime, received Reynolds with courtesy. The challenge to a duel was issued and was accepted by the Frenchman. In deference to Shelby's stiff right wrist, which made the use of the sword impossible, Preuil graciously and chivalrously chose pistols at ten paces. The duel would be fought at daylight the next morning.

But neither would-be principal visited the field of honor at the appointed hour. A short time after the challenge had been issued and accepted, Colonel Jeanningros, on a quick tour of inspection of his department and accompanied by four squadrons of Chasseurs d'Afrique, rode into Parras. He soon heard the details of Shelby's interview with Preuil and of Preuil's treatment of the Southern officer. He quickly forbade the duel and placed the Colonel under arrest until he apologized to Shelby for his discourteous treatment. The next morning Preuil visited Shelby and apologized, for he sincerely regretted his drunken and discourteous action of the preceding night.

That Shelby completely forgave him was proven a year later. At that time Preuil was commanding an isolated post north of Queretero and a detachment of the Liberal Army was rapidly closing around him. He did not have the strength to withstand their attack. Shelby was freighting goods in the vicinity when he heard of the plight of his erstwhile enemy. Without hesitation he secured some forty volunteers, rode a little over one hundred and sixty miles in twenty-six hours and saved Preuil and his garrison.

From Colonel Jeanningros Shelby discovered that Bazaine had indeed ordered him to turn away from Sonora and the Pacific ports and report to the City of Mexico. While he could not understand this sudden turn of events, Shelby realized that he would gain nothing by refusing to obey the command of the French marshal who controlled the military power of the Empire. It was possible that Bazaine had plans for the enlistment of his men into the active service of the Emperor. The men had voted for Maximilian and Carlota. They would march to the capital.

The men heard the news of the change in plans with enthusiasm. Who, after all, wanted to march the long weary miles across northern Mexico to Mazatlan or Guaymas? It was nearly five hundred miles to Mazatlan and nearly seven hundred miles to Guaymas, and the entire route to both places was across a desert burning with the summer's heat. It was nearly six hundred miles to the capital but only two hundred and fifty miles of the distance would be over the cactus and mesquite covered desert; south of Las Bocas (thirty miles north of San Luis Potosi) they would enter the heartland of Mexico and the march would be one long holiday through San Luis Potosi, Dolores Hidalgo, San Miguel de Allende, Queretaro, and other towns where there would be *fiestas* and perhaps love-making on moonlit nights. And then the capital, the City of Mexico, the City of the Palaces, the most fabulous city in the Western Hemisphere, the seat of the Empire.

That night they dreamed of the Alameda and the great square in front of the National Palace and the floating islands of Xochimilco, as marvelous as the hanging gardens of Babylon, and the castle atop Chapultepec, the Hill of the Grasshoppers, the castle where dwelt Carlota, the Empress they had chosen to serve.

VI

SOUTHWARD
TO QUERETARO

16. La Encarnacion

THE BRIGADE rode out from Parras and into the broad
valley which ran southeastward. For the next sixty-five
miles, until La Encantada was reached, it would retrace
the route over which it had marched from Saltillo and the battlefield of Buena Vista.

The troopers rode deep, as the old cavalry saying went, their
feet thrust solidly through the stirrups, their bodies well settled
between the cantles and the horns of their saddles. Reins were
held loosely, for the pace was slow and the horses accustomed to
following the column. At the head of the file the guidon fluttered
lazily in the quiet morning air. Today would be the same as
other days on the march, and tomorrow would be the same as
today and the day after. Once the valley was left behind, the
route to San Luis Potosi would traverse a dry and sterile country,
hot by day and cold by night, and monotony would eat into
the men with all the persistence of the slow, repetitious rains
which fell during the rainy season to erode the red and copper
hills stretching away into the horizon on either side.

But the valley was rich with growing things; better enjoy it
while you can, soldier. On its floor and the lower slopes of the
sierras were checkerboarded fields of maguey, corn, and small
grains, orchards of pears, apples, peaches, olives and Indian figs,
and vineyards of Spanish uva vines for which Parras was noted.

Villages were frequent, nestled among the trees that lined the
small streams which came tumbling down from the heights on
either side, and their general patterns were the same—a single
street of one-story, flat-roofed, adobe houses, with the ceiling
rafters projecting a foot or more through the walls; the little
square or plaza with the ever-present church on one side; horses

119

or burros standing idly, with lowered heads, in the heat of the sun; ox-drawn *carretas*—huge, clumsy, two-wheeled carts that squeaked with a high-pitched sound; a few lounging *vaqueros* or *caballeros* or *peons* leaning against the walls; and dogs and children—each village was filled with them and it was difficult to determine which made the more noise. Except for their names— Cuevas, San Miguel, La Paz, San Blas, Derramadero, El Jaral— the villages were all alike.

The Brigade reached La Encantada, a few miles south of the Buena Vista battlefield, through which it had passed but a few days before. From La Encantada the route drove straight southward for over two hundred miles to San Luis Potosi.

The country here was cold, for the altitude at La Encantada was just over six thousand feet; it rose still higher at Agua Nueva, and climbed to a seventy-three hundred foot pass at Los Carneros. But the horses had become acclimated to the higher altitudes on the march to Monterrey and the warm summer had tempered the frigid winds. The camp just south of Los Carneros was not unpleasant.

Yandell Blackwell and James Wood stood guard duty at one of the advanced posts and, as their little campfire smouldered fitfully, lost themselves in the quiet reverie of the night. Only the usual sounds were heard—calls of birds that flew in the darkness, buzzing of ever-present insects, and, off in the distance, the high-pitched yapping of coyotes. The two men sat at their fire, which had been built in a small depression so that their silhouettes would not show against the skyline.

Suddenly a noise was heard and the men flattened on the ground and peered into the darkness. A man was approaching, waving in front of him a blanket as a sort of flag of truce. He came up to the fire and sat down. Indian like, he waited a few moments before speaking. Then a question—had the *Americanos* heard of La Encarnacion?

They had heard that it was a small village. They would pass through it within a few days perhaps.

No, he did not refer to the village. He referred to the Hacienda de la Encarnacion and to the *hacendado,* Don Luis Enrico Rodriguez.

They had not heard of the *hacienda* or of the owner.

120

Did the *Americanos* have the time—it would take only a few of their precious minutes—to listen to a story? Perhaps it would interest them. *Quien sabe?* At any rate it concerned one of their countrywomen.

Don Luis was a Spaniard who had bought the *hacienda* some years before. How or where he got the money was not known, but certainly it was not like him to have worked for it. He had enlarged this *hacienda* until it was a great landed estate with a fine house built inside high and thick walls which enclosed a vast number of buildings. Perhaps when the night was dark and the bats—who were the minions of the Devil—flew about the Don was not the pleasant, open-hearted man he appeared to be when noted or wealthy travelers sought lodging at his house or soldiers camped just outside his walls. Perhaps he consorted with robbers and bandits, and so made more *pesos* in this way than he did with his maguey and his maize and his cattle and horses. That he was a devil incarnate everyone knew, not only from the beatings he gave his *peons* and the numbers of easy-virtued *señoritas* who thronged his estate, but from the fact that he tried to keep hidden from prying eyes a faded, prematurely-aged American woman.

They had never heard of her? This soft-spoken, white-haired lady of blasted beauty, whom the servants called a spirit from Heaven and the lazy, aged gossips a *Gringa*. This kindly lady who had been kidnapped and stolen from her father by Don Luis? This lady who was called Inez Walker?

Blackwell and Wood shook their heads. They did not trust the man, so they grasped their revolvers a bit more tightly and bade him continue.

The Mexican crossed himself and muttered a prayer. That he himself feared Don Luis was obvious, but the fear had not paralyzed his tongue. Perhaps the woman had befriended him in days past; perhaps he was only trying to help the *Señor* who was in the sky. Blackwell and Wood wondered.

Years ago an *Americano* had come from the North to hunt for gold in Sonora. He had searched in the mountains and in the *arroyos* and *barrancas*. He had not stolen from the Indians and had divided his food with them. They had grown friendly with him and had taken him home with them to the brush

121

jacales of their villages. There he had met and married one of the daughters of the tribe, and later they had had a daughter. The *Americano* had found gold (perhaps the Indians had shown him where it was). He had become a wealthy man and had built a big house in Guaymas where he lived as all rich men live. He had sent the daughter to California, and she had been educated as a lady, a grand *señorita,* for she was the daughter of a rich man.

By the time she returned from her schooling she had become a beautiful young woman, with all the dark loveliness of her mother's people and the blond hair of her father. But she was no longer Mexican, she was an *Americana,* for she had forgotten how to speak with the father and the mother of her mother and their people. She dressed as a foreigner and she no longer ate *tortillas* and *frijoles* and *carnes caliente* as she had done when she was a little girl. Yes, she had become a *Gringa.*

Then one day Don Luis had gone to Guaymas and there had seen her. His desire had been immediate and all consuming. He had paid court to her, sent flowers and sweetmeats, dressed in his best and called on her family. He was a Spaniard, *Señores,* a rich Spaniard, and to a rich Spaniard the possessing of everything that is desired is but a matter of time.

But the young lady had had nothing to do with him, though he had pled long and ardently with her. He had failed with his money and with his impassioned entreaties; he had failed in his attempts to impress her with his social position and with the little strategems that all lovers are well acquainted with.

Then he had grown angry and bitter. He would have her. How? It was simple. One night he had gathered about him a group of his bandits and cut-throats and had carried her off. Her father had given pursuit, caught up with the thieves and in the foray that followed had been killed.

Don Luis had carried the beautiful Inez to his *hacienda* at La Encarnacion. There she was the mistress of a great estate. Servants came at her bidding, fine costumes were ordered for her from the City of Mexico, exotic and delicious foods arrived from the far corners of the country, priests fawned upon and blessed her. But she had not relented. Don Luis had pled and begged and implored. By turns he had gone into towering rages

122

Maximilian I, Emperor of Mexico.

and humbling repentances when he groveled in the dust at her feet.

Señorita Inez had still refused him, for she constantly envisioned him as the murderer of her father, called him murdered to his face and to his face prayed for vengeance. Her body had wasted, her hair had turned gray. Her mind had begun to wander and sometimes at night her servants had heard awful and pitiful cries coming from her room, and at such times they had crossed themselves and said an Ave Maria. Once, during a storm, she had escaped but had been found and carried back to her prison. This incident had broken her spirit but she had lived on, a half-demented, fragile, skeleton-like creature in a nether world of light and shadow.

The *peon* goatherd paused. The nearly-spent campfire threw fluttering light patches across his dark face. In a lonely cavalry outpost in the highlands of central Mexico a lowly Mexican had told the story of an American's daughter to two Americans' sons.

Neither Wood nor Blackwell had moved. Then Wood, without turning his head and still staring vaguely off into the dark-

123

ness, said, "Is it far to Encarnacion?" The words came haltingly, for Spanish was an unfamiliar tongue.

"By to-morrow night, *Señor,* you will be there."

"Have you told the straight truth, Mexican?"

"As the Virgin is true, *Señor.*"

"So be it. You will sleep this night at the outpost. To-morrow we shall see."

The *peon* rolled and smoked a cigarette. Then he wrapped himself in the serape and lay down. Whether or not he slept neither Wood nor Blackwell knew, but he never moved. Undoubtedly he was an Indian. Did Indians ever sleep?

The two guards rebuilt their fire and sat for an hour or more in silence. Finally Blackwell spoke: "Of what are you thinking?"

"Encarnacion. And you?"

"Inez Walker. It is the same."

The Indian stirred. Instantly the revolvers covered him. "Lie still," said Wood, "and muffle up your ears. You may not understand English, but you understand this." And he stuck the pistol into his face. When daylight came neither Wood nor Blackwell had unfolded his blanket.

The Brigade moved out as usual that morning and late in the afternoon came to the village of La Encarnacion. A short distance away stood the *hacienda* of Don Luis Rodriguez. Camp was made without incident, but Shelby observed that Don Luis did not visit him, which was contrary to the custom of the country. He also noticed that scattered groups of *vaqueros* and *rancheros,* clad in their tight fitting, flaring-legged trousers, with stripes of ornamented leather running down the sides from the knees, their short jackets, and their broad-brimmed, high-crowned leather hats banded with gold or silver, had ridden through the great gate of the *hacienda* upon their richly caparisoned horses.

"They do not come out," Shelby said. "There are some signs of preparation about." He ordered the night guard strengthened.

Blackwell and Wood had discussed the plight of Inez Walker during the day and had decided to rescue the American woman. They invited some of their comrades to accompany them and eighteen responded to the call. Wood was the leader and twice he had been at the point of telling Shelby the whole story, but

Shelby had tightened discipline considerably since they had left Parras and he was in no mood for dangerous and unnecessary heroics. Perhaps it would be best not to tell him. Wood kept his own counsel.

As the pickets were forming to go to their night posts, Wood walked over to Blackwell. "The men will be ready by twelve. They are volunteers and splendid fellows. How many of them will be shot?"

"*Quien sabe?* Those who take the sword shall perish by the sword."

"Bah! When you take a text, take one without a woman in it."

"I shall not preach to-night. Shelby will do that tomorrow to all who come forth scathless."

One by one the volunteers stole away from the sleeping camp and gathered at an outer picket post. There was no watch word that night and the men were free to come and go as they chose. By midnight the twenty men were ready; all members of the Old Brigade, including Tom Rudd, Dick Collins, Dick and Isaac Berry and Crockett, who had fought the knife duel at Lampazos.

Wood spoke to them: "Boys, none of us know what is waiting inside the corral. Mexicans fight well in the dark, it is said, and see better than wolves, but we must have that American woman safe out of their hands, or we must burn the buildings. If the hazard is too great for any of you, step out of the ranks. What we are about to do must needs be done quickly."

He paused.

"Shelby sleeps little of late, and may be, even at this very moment, searching through the camp for some of us. Let him find, even so much as one blanket empty, and from the heroes of a night attack we shall become its criminals."

Sweeny, one of the bravest of the Old Brigade, who was one-armed and who had soldiered with the noted filibuster William Walker in Nicaragua in the middle 1850's, replied to Wood: "Since time is valuable, lead on."

The men filed off toward the *hacienda,* two of them serving as an advance guard to try the main gate. They found it unguarded but locked and hurried back to report.

125

"It is dark all about there, and the gate itself is as strong as a mountain."

"We shall batter it down."

After continued searching, they found a huge timber at one of the irrigation gates and carried it up the slope.

A light glowed from the top of the high watchtower that flanked the main building, but the high walls that encircled the mansion, houses of laborers and servants, stables, sheds, and other buildings, prevented light from reaching the immediate outside of the wall.

They reached the gate and listened. Nothing could be heard but the rustle of the acacia leaves and the plaintive splashing of the fountain inside the walls. They examined the gate and found the vulnerable point near the lock. Backing away in order to gain momentum, they charged the gate with their heavy battering-ram. There was a loud crash and they went through. Dropping the timber, they ran for the mansion alongside the tower.

The din rose—yells of the men, rearing and neighing of corralled horses, barking of dogs; then a united yell from a score of Mexicans who had been sleeping on their flank near the corral. With a dozen men, Macey and Berry turned and charged them, while the rest continued toward the house. A solid sheet of flame broke from the corral but the men swept through and completed their work. Meantime Wood and his group had been hammering on the massive door of the mansion.

They heard the shrill blare of a bugle from Shelby's camp, and Wood yelled: "Make haste! make haste, men, for in twenty minutes we will be between two fires."

Every Mexican outside the house had been killed, but the front door still held. Rodriguez showed himself for a moment on the tower and a dozen men fired as he ducked and yelled defiance at them. From the windows and the roof top came intermittent flashes of gun fire. Then the door crashed and the men poured into the house.

Now it was a furious hurricane of fighting within the rooms, fighting in total darkness in which the Americans only recognized their comrades by their piercing Rebel yells. Crockett, the duelist, was killed, and young Tom Rudd, and Rogers. Provines, who was just a boy, lay lifeless on the floor and Matterhorn, the huge German giant, received four bullets and lay dying.

They reached the great hall of the *hacienda* but its door held against them. The battering ram was brought up and they went through with a splintering of wood. Now there was hand-to-hand killing again and at last the Mexicans broke and tried to flee the holocaust. Some escaped but many were cut down as they crossed the courtyard.

The men found candles and lamps and lighted them. The room was littered with dead men who lay grotesquely where they had fallen. Over in one corner lay the body of Don Luis. No one knew who had killed him, and no one cared. Trembling servants appeared and were sent scurrying for bandages and water for the wounded.

Then Shelby came striding into the great hall, his face red with anger, his mouth twitching. His men had attacked the *hacienda*. What other reason than for plunder?

"Who among you have done this thing?"

There was no reply as the men slowly holstered their revolvers, wiped and put away their knives.

"Speak, some of you. Let me not find cowards instead of plunderers, lest I finish the work upon you all that the Mexicans did so poorly upon a few."

Jim Wood came forward and told the story just as he and Blackwell had heard it from the *peon* herder. Jo Shelby's anger cooled as Wood told the story. Whether or not it was because so many of the Old Brigade were involved or that the romantic nature of the bloody adventure appealed to him the men never knew, but they could see his face gradually lose its hardness.

When he finally spoke he said, "And where is the woman?"

During the battle Inez Walker had been forgotten. A servant was sent to bring her from her room.

John Edwards described her entrance in his usual romantic fashion: "Grief-stricken, prematurely old, yet beautiful even amid the loneliness of her situation, Inez Walker came into the presence of Shelby, a queen. Some strands of gray were in her glossy, golden hair. The liquid light of her large dark eyes had long ago been quenched in tears. The form that had once been so full and perfect, was now bent and fragile; but there was such

127

a look of mournful tenderness in her eager, questioning face that the men drew back from her presence instinctively and left her alone with their General."

Shelby "received her commands as if she were bestowing a favor upon him, listening as a brother might until all her wishes were made known." He promised to respect her wishes regarding her dead and to conduct her safely to the City of Mexico; from there she could return to Sonora or go to the United States.

The next morning the Brigade continued its march toward San Luis Potosi and accompanying it was a closed carriage, a sort of *diligencia,* flanked by a guard of honor.

17. Rescue of the Garrison at Matehuala

THE BRIGADE moved southward from the heights of Carnero Pass onto a broad, arid plain, bordered on either side by lofty, bare sierras. Except for a few small grains which matured quickly during the rainy season, irrigation was necessary for the production of crops, and tanks and ponds were numerous. In unirrigated areas there was little vegetation except *huisachi, mesquite* and shrub-palms.

They passed large *haciendas* and *ranchos,* with their unified clusters of buildings surrounded by the ever-present high wall and with their low, boundary line fences of stone running straight up the slopes to the mountain heights. They skirted the Hacienda del Salado, one of the largest in northern Mexico, which produced thousands of horses and cattle yearly and skirted Cedral, a small village set in bleak hills, from which came silver and sulphur and which was towered over by a great pyramidal mountain called El Fraile, the Monk. At Cedral the plain broadened, then closed again as the blue limestone mountains of Catorce were reached. The water here was slightly purgative and was drunk sparingly by man and beast.

They made slow time as they approached Matehuala, for the road worked its way upward through foothills, then into mountains where the grades were sharp and the road narrowed into a trail only wide enough for a column of twos. Late in the afternoon as they neared the town they suddenly heard the sound of small arms fire and the deep, heavy rumble of artillery. Scouts moved forward and brought back word that the town was under siege.

Shelby halted until night fell, then moved the Brigade to within about two miles of the besieging lines, which were drawn close and tight around the beleaguered French. He detailed four detachments under Kirtley, Collins, Macey and Dorsey, with fifteen men each, to fan out, half circle Matehuala and bring back such information as they could. Macey made a wide detour to the left and down into the valley, passed through a village, captured and brought back five prisoners. Kirtley continued on the main road until he ran into a large number of troops in bivouac. Collins and Dorsey also ran into troops and Collins had to fight a sharp little engagement before cutting his way out of a company of cavalry.

Shelby talked to the prisoners and from them learned that Major Henri Pierron, a youthful and dauntless French officer, held the town with five hundred of the 82nd Infantry of the Line. He was besieged by about two thousand Liberals and guerrillas under the nominal command of General Mariano Escobedo. The garrison was small for such an exposed outpost and in all probability would be overwhelmed when the grand attack was made the next morning.

Shelby called his men together. "We have marched far, we have but scant money, our horses are footsore and much in need of shoes, and Matehuala is across the only road for scores of miles in any direction that leads to Mexico. Shall we turn back and take another."

The men were tired of marching, wanted rest and relaxation. They had no intention of turning back.

"But there are two thousand Mexican soldiers, or robbers, . . . across this road, and we may have to fight a little. Are you tired of fighting."

"Lead us on and see," was the reply. They realized that he was tempting them and that he had already decided to attack the besiegers at daylight the next morning. This suited them perfectly. There was no discussion.

"One other thing," said Shelby, "before we separate. From among you I want a couple of volunteers—two men who will

129

take their lives in their hands and find an entrance into Matehuala. I must communicate with Pierron before daylight. It is
necessary that he should know how near there is succor to him,
and how furiously we mean to charge them in the morning. Who
will go?"

From the volunteers Shelby chose James Cundiff and Elias
Hodge. While not proficient in Spanish, they had learned enough
since entering Mexico to make simple wants known; it was not
enough, however, to pass themselves off in the dark as two
Mexicans.

They asked about the message they would take to Pierron
but Shelby refused to write one. "A document might hang
you," he said, "and besides, Pierron cannot, in all probability,
read my English. Go, and may God protect you." The two men
disappeared into the windy and cloudy night, which favored
their venture, for the winds covered the sounds of their foot-
steps and the darkness hid them from night prowlers and organized pickets.

They moved off by the left flank to make a wide detour
into the town, for the main road was blocked by the Liberals
and the right flank was difficult because of the mountainous
character of the terrain, and proceeded carefully in single file,
pausing frequently to listen. They were experienced scouts; for
the past four years they had campaigned in Arkansas and Missouri and Shelby was a leader who liked to know the exact
position of the enemy whenever possible.

Coming down from the hills, they entered the valley and
passed through plowed fields crisscrossed with irrigation ditches
which made rapid movement impossible. They occasionally ran
into cactus fences and corrals, or houses which had to be carefully skirted for fear of watchful dogs. They finally found a road
and continued along it until they came to a small village alive
with soldiers.

"They are here," said Hodge.

"They seem to be everywhere," answered Cundiff.

"What do you propose?"

"To glide quietly through. I have a strong belief that beyond
this village we shall find Matehuala."

They struck out again, moving carefully and slowly, for it

would be difficult to escape detection. Then fortune moved against them. The sound of moving horses came from down the road. Instantly they moved off to the side behind a huge maguey plant and waited. The horsemen came on unsuspectingly and passed within a few feet of the crouching scouts.

"A scratch," said Hodge.

"Hush," said Cundiff, "The worst is yet to come."

They were only about fifty feet from a *cantina,* ablaze with light and from which came the sounds of revelry. Those within heard the horsemen and poured from the building, yelled for identification of the retreating riders and when none was given ran to their horses. The half-drunken men spread out like a fan and began to search the darkness. A small group rode up the road toward Hodge and Cundiff.

"There are five," said Hodge, "and we are but two. We have fought worse odds."

"So we have," Cundiff replied, "and may do it again before this night's work is over. Lie low and wait."

The soldiers came on. Suddenly the nearest turned and saw them: "What ho! comrades, close up—close up—here are two skulking Frenchmen."

He leveled his musket but Cundiff dropped him from his horse while Hodge wounded one of the other; then they fled across an open field toward Matehuala.

"This pace is fearful. How long can you keep it up?" said Cundiff after a few minutes of running over the broken and uneven ground.

"Not long. There seems, however, to be a light ahead."

They saw a large fire about five hundred yards in front of them and men rushing to and fro about it. Then there came the blare of a bugle and the men formed into line. Was it a French outpost or was it a camp of the besieging army?

"We are surrounded," panted Hodge.

"Rather say we are in the breakers," replied Cundiff, as he turned and snapped a shot at their pursuers. "It all depends upon a single chance."

"And what is that chance?"

"To escape the first close fusillade of the French."

"But are they French—those fellows in front of us?"

131

"Can't you swear to that? Did you not mark how accurately they fell into line, and how silent everything has been since? Keep your ears wide upon and when you hear a single voice call out fall flat upon the ground for that single voice will be the order for a volley."

Hodge and Cundiff ran on toward the outpost, pausing every few yards to turn and fire upon their pursuers, who, after their first shots, kept a safe distance behind, making no effort to close the interval.

"Come," Cundiff called out, "and let's try the unknown. These fellows in the rear have had enough."

They continued toward the French line, Hodge on one side of the road and Cundiff on the other in skirmishing order. The French officer's sharp command rang out and the men dropped to the ground as the volley came.

Hodge yelled out, "Hold on, men, hold on. We are but two and we are friends. See, we come into your lines to make our words good. We are Americans and we have information for Major Pierron."

They were conducted to Major Pierron and informed him of Shelby's plans for the relief of the garrison. At the conclusion of the conference, Cundiff said, "We must return."

Pierron glanced at the two Americans in surprise, "Return, the devil! You have not said your prayers yet for being permitted to get in."

"No matter. He prays best who fights the best, and Shelby gives no thanks for unfinished work. Am I right, Hodge?"

"Now as always; but surely Major Pierron can send us by a nearer road."

Pierron conferred with his officers. Undoubtedly this American would keep his word and break through the besieging lines the next morning. Why not send some Cuirassiers to guide the scouts back with their report in order that the attack might be coordinated with a sortie by the besieged garrison? The Mexicans would not attempt to block them, for their departure would weaken an already weak garrison. So forty Cuirassiers rode with Hodge and Cundiff out of Matehuala and by daylight had arrived at Shelby's camp.

Shelby laid his plans while the men got ready for battle, the last engagement they were to fight as an organized force. Excited by the accounts of Hodge and Cundiff, they checked guns, revolvers and other equipment as they had done a hundred times during the war.

The Mexican siege guns had opened up on Matehuala about daylight and their infantry lines were moving forward as Shelby and his men rode down the winding, wooded slopes from the mountains. As they broke into view the Mexicans wondered if they were friend or foe, but relaxed at the sight of their strange guidon. This was certainly no squadron of Frenchmen coming to the relief of the garrison. If not Frenchmen, they must be friends.

In planning the battle, Shelby had reverted to one of the old methods of attack which had been so successful back in Arkansas and Missouri. His force would move forward by companies in a column of fours at the walk, then the trot, then the canter, and finally at the whirlwind charge, using first the revolver and then the sword. The solid, single column would fan out by companies as the Mexican lines were penetrated. Except for the recruits that had been enlisted in Texas, it was old work and the new men would keep ranks with the others.

The Brigade came to the open fields and advanced to the trot. Shelby rode some distance ahead of the first company. Maurice Langhorne came galloping up, Langhorne who had led many a desperate charge during the old days, but Shelby stopped him with a wave of the hand, "We know what is before us," he said, "and it is my pleasure this morning to receive the fire first of you all. Take your place with your company, the fifth from the front."

Then Shelby raised his arm and shouted, "Gallop—Ho!" And the arm went forward and down in the old cavalry signal.

The Mexican forces were drawn up before them, three lines deep, with a heavy six-gun battery. Shelby aimed his attack at the battery. At the same moment the French lines rose and charged forward while their cavalry rode along the flanks. The Mexicans suddenly realized that they were neatly caught between two fires. They hesitated, paralyzed for the moment; then it was too late.

The Brigade hit them and carried everything before it, went

133

right through at the furious charge, then wheeled for the counter stroke. The battery had only dead and wounded men around it and the lines were broken; the revolvers had done their work, now for the sabres. Men threw down their arms, screamed and tried to run, only to be cut down by strokes that endlessly rose and fell. The field became a slaughterhouse as the French Cuirassiers dashed in from the flanks.

A smoke pall lay over the plowed fields of dead and dying. The besieging Mexican army was scattered and demoralized, while the Cuirassiers mopped up the little groups that here and there huddled together and tried to make a stand.

Major Pierron rode up to Shelby, thanked him for his timely assistance and conducted the Brigade into Matehuala.

18. The Last Adventures

JOHN EDWARDS wrote with fond recollection of those days in Matehuala: "Pierron made Matehuala a paradise. There were days of feasting and mirth and minstrelsy, and in the balm of fragrant nights the men dallied with the women. So when the southward march was resumed, many a bronzed face was set in a look of sadness, and many a regretful heart pined long and tenderly for the dusky hair that would never be plaited again, for the tropical lips that for them would never sing again the songs of roses and the summer time."

The Brigade moved off toward San Luis Potosi, which lay about a hundred and thirty miles southward. It angled west a few miles and passed through the village of Catorce, which means "fourteen" and which had been named for a band of fourteen bandits who once had terrorized the area, then turned south and proceeded along the high tableland that is central Mexico. To the eastward rose the high mountains of the Sierra Madre Oriental, to the westward the plain gradually merged into gently rolling country. The climate even in summer was invigorating, for the altitude reached over six thousand feet, and the nights were cold, but the land was generally arid and dotted with *mesquite* and *maguey* and *nopal*.

Laguna Seca, with its paradisiacal Hacienda de Solis, Charcas and Venado and Las Bocas, which boasted a large lake and

134

Hacienda de Solis, southwest of Matehuala.

fine gardens, were left behind. The brown stone towers of the Cathedral of San Luis Potosi came into view, a sizable city and a silver mining center lying in the midst of a broad, flat plain with only a few trees to break the monotony of the distant horizons.

The French garrison at San Luis Potosi was commanded by General Felix Douay, an old soldier who was a close confidant of Bazaine. A tall, gaunt man past sixty years of age, he had spent his entire life in the army and had served in many countries. He sent for Shelby.

"You have come among us for an object," he said in perfect English, "and as I am a man of few words, please state to me frankly what that object is."

"To take service under Maximilian."

"What are your facilities for recruiting a corps of Americans?"

"So ample, General, that if authority is given me, I can pledge to you the services of fifty thousand in six months." Despite his disappointments in Texas and in Northern Mexico, Shelby was still confident.

135

"You will remain here until further orders. It may be that there shall be work for your hands sooner than either of us expect."

Douay dispatched a messenger to the City of Mexico with the request that the Americans might be enlisted in the services of the Emperor and sent against the bandit chieftain—Liberal General Luis Perez Figueroa in the lowlands of southern Tamaupilas, northern Vera Cruz and eastern San Luis Potosi, along the Tamesin, Verde, Santa Maria, and Panuco rivers.

Figueroa was somewhat past forty-five years of age, taller than most of his nationality, and was one-eyed from the bullet of an American revolver, which caused most of his hatred of foreigners to be concentrated on them. He was typical of many such chieftains operating in Mexico at the time, Mexicans who nominally allied themselves with Juarez, but who robbed and plundered and murdered when not engaged in leading minor forays against Bazaine or the Royalists. But of all of them— Rodriguez the renegade priest, Lozado the Indian, Cortina, Martinez, Carabajal, Escobedo—Figueroa had no peer. He delighted in the plunder and butchery of peaceful *peon* non-combatants who had not taken sides in the political struggle that now engulfed Mexico and who only wished to till their little *milpas* in peace.

Douay had sent several expeditions—Chasseurs of Vincennes, Voltigeurs, the Foreign Legion, even the Zouaves—against the guerrillas, but with no success. They had been defeated, not by Figueroa, but by the marshes and the swamps, their reptiles and the dreaded tropical *vomito* that lurked in the long lagoons and sluggish mosquito-infested rivers. On two occasions Dupin and his dreaded Contre-Guerrillas had brought Figueroa to bay, but on each occasion he had escaped into the jungle. Figueroa continued to cut the line of communication between San Luis Potosi and Tampico. His forces must be dispersed if the arms of France were to succeed in pacifying Maximilian's Empire.

So followed a few days of waiting and pleasure for the Brigade until Bazaine's decision was received. When it finally came it was laconic and to the point: "Bid the Americans march immediately to Mexico."

The first day's march brought the expedition to the Hacienda

Plaza and cathedral at San Luis Potosi.

de Jorol, once one of the largest in Mexico, larger even than the state of Delaware, where, before the Revolution, the Spanish noble *hacendado* had had 30,000 retainers and had grazed over 300,000 head of livestock. Now the estate bore the marks of decay and dilapidation.

On the third day out of San Luis Potosi the ambulance, which carried two wounded soldiers, broke down. The accident occurred as the Brigade was passing over the divide of one of the short mountain ranges which crisscross the central region of Mexico in a wild and rough country. The rearguard had the ambulance in its charge and followed the main body into the night's camp. When Shelby came to see the wounded men and the ambulance was not there, he called for the officer in command and asked its whereabouts.

"It is in Sumapetla."

"And the wounded?"

"At a house with one attendant."

Realizing instantly the dangerous position of the wounded men

137

in a country filled with guerrillas and bandits, Shelby's face angered.

"If a hair of either head is touched," he said, "it will be better that you had never crossed the Rio Grande. What avails all the lessons you have learned of this treacherous and deceitful land that you should desert comrades in distress and ride up to tell me the pleasant story of your own arrival and safety? Order Kirtley to report instantly with twenty men."

James Kirtley, the smooth-faced young officer, soon reported. Shelby's order was brief and tersely given: "Return to Sumapetla and find my wounded. Stay with them, wait for them, fight for them, get killed, if need be, for them, but whatever you do, bring or send them back to me. I shall wait for you a day and a night."

By this time it was dark and it was ten miles back to Sumapetla. Kirtley asked for volunteers, selected twenty men, and was off at a gallop. He called out to his men: "Keep quiet, be ready, be loaded. You heard the orders."

Kirtley found the two wounded men at the best house in the village and the attendant, who had been a blacksmith before the war, busily engaged in repairing the ambulance. He threw a picket guard of five men a short distance beyond the village and stationed the rest in the shadows of the houses.

It was not long before a vicious volley poured in on the pickets. One of them rode back and reported to Kirtley; "There is a large body in front of us and well armed. They tried a surprise and lost five. We did not think it well to charge, and I have come back for orders. Please say what they are quick, for the boys may need me before I can reach them again." It was the officer of the rearguard who had abandoned the two wounded men earlier that day.

Kirtley's remaining fifteen men rode rapidly forward. He ordered the pickets to fall back some fifteen or twenty yards to a curve in the road where a cluster of jagged rocks provided a good defensive position. Here the force settled down to await attack. Meantime the blacksmith reported that it would be two hours before the ambulance was repaired.

Another volley poured from the darkness and a man fell. Kirtley called out, "Who's hurt?"

"It's me, Jim; it's Walker. Hard hit in the shoulder; but thank God for the breech loader, a fellow can load and fire with one sound arm left." Walker crawled back to his position and resumed his post.

The minutes slowly ate into the two hours. By that time nine of the men had been wounded, although only one of them, Walker, seriously. When the ambulance was ready to move Kirtley said to William Fell, who was standing near, "It can travel but slowly in the night and we must paralyze pursuit a little."

"Paralyze it—how?"

"By a sudden blow, such as a prize fighter gives when he strikes below the belt. By a charge some good hundred paces in the midst of them."

"Desperate but reasonable. I have seen such things done."

Kirtley said, almost to himself, "There will be but eleven of us. The nine who are wounded must go back."

The horses were brought up and the wounded men ordered to accompany the ambulance. They were helped on their horses and two of them rode with Walker, half holding him in the saddle.

The others waited for the signal, then rode up the road toward the bandits, broke their line and went through. Then, wheeling, they came back. Not a man was hit. The necessary diversion for the escape of the ambulance had been secured. By sunup the rescuing party with its wounded had reached Shelby's camp.

A day or two later the Brigade moved on to Dolores Hidalgo, where it remained until the more seriously wounded were able to continue the march to the City of Mexico. Dolores was a good sized town where Father Hidalgo, one of the leaders of the Mexican Revolution, had been born and where he had given his famous *Grito* (cry) of Independence, "Long live our Lady of Guadalupe! Long live Independence!" back in 1810.

One evening word was brought to Shelby that a detachment of ten men were refusing guard duty and sitting around their campfire awaiting supper.

"They refuse?" asked Shelby, incredulously.

"Peremptorily, General."

"Ah! And for what reason?"

"They say it is unnecessary."

139

"And so, in addition to rank mutiny, they would justify themselves? Call out the guard!"

Shelby hurried over to the mutineers. "Men," he said quietly, "go back to your duty. I am among you all, an adventurer like yourself, but I have been charged to carry you through to Mexico City in safety, and this I will do, so surely as the good God rules the universe. I don't seek to know the cause of this thing. I ask no reason for it, no excuse for it, no regrets nor apologies for it. I only want your soldierly promise to obey."

For a moment no one spoke and no one moved. Then the leader stood up and started to advance, but Shelby stopped him with a gesture, "Not another word, but if within fifteen seconds by the watch you are not in line for duty, you shall be shot like the meanest dog in all the Empire. Cover these men, Macey, with your carbines."

Within a few moments the men were at their posts. Thereafter, until the Brigade reached the City of Mexico, although they were passing through country well patrolled by the French, Shelby's discipline noticeably tightened; there was no more thought of mutiny.

One day Shelby and his men moved out from Dolores Hidalgo along the twenty-five mile road to San Miguel de Allende. Some ten or twelve miles south they passed through Jesus Nazareno de Atotonilco, the village where Father Hidalgo first took the banner of the Virgin of Guadalupe as the battle standard of Independence. It was a beautiful country, the Valley of Laja, with rich farms and *haciendas,* green fields and their grazing horses and cattle, through which ran clear, sparkling streams bridged with ancient and fanciful arches of stone that bespoke pride in the building.

Late in the afternoon, Dick Collins and Ike Berry, dusty and tired, fell out of the rearguard for a short rest. They were well aware of the fact that they were disobeying orders. Oh, well, they would only rest a little while, they would soon catch up. But their good intentions were never realized for they lay back upon the grass and were soon asleep.

A half dozen wandering guerrillas found them and before they could reach for their revolvers felled Berry with the butt of a musquetoon and Collins with the back of a sword. Disarmed,

140

they stood before their captors, who were dressed in the ornate and fanciful costume of Mexican *Charros*—with elaborately decorated and ornamented tight-fitting pants, pointed-toed riding boots, silvered spurs, short jackets and gay *sombreros*.

"*Françaises,* eh?" they questioned.

"No, no, *Señores,* not *Françaises* but *Americanos.*" Berry and Collins knew that unless they convinced their captors that they were not Frenchmen that they would be speedily murdered. They did their best, with such Spanish words as they knew.

They were carried across the country a few miles into the foothills to a cluster of low adobe buildings and thrown into a small, windowless room. Two guards sat in the doorway.

"What are you thinking about, Dick?" asked Berry.

"Escape. And you?"

"Of something to eat." The Hercules who was always hungry was not out of character, even when sitting a prisoner in a dirty, flea-ridden hut in Central Mexico with little prospect of living out the day.

The afternoon wore on and night came. After supper the guards drank more wine than was good for them and finally one of them, who had a knife sticking out of the sash at his waist, tumbled over in peaceful, drunken slumber, while the other amused himself by pointing his musquetoon at Berry and Collins and cocking the hammer.

Then Collins whispered out of the corner of his mouth at Berry, "You are as strong as an ox. Stand by me when I seize that knife and plunge it in the other Mexican's breast. I may not kill him the first time, and if I do not, then grapple with him. The second stab shall be more fatal."

"Unto death," murmured Berry. "Make haste."

Waiting until the eyes of the guard moved momentarily from them, Collins stole across the room, seized the knife and leaped. The guard heard him, looked up and raised his gun, but it was too late.

The two men stripped the Mexicans of their weapons, found their horses unguarded and rode into the night. By noon the next day they had caught up with the column. No one straggled again.

The spires of San Miguel de Allende finally came into view

141

and the Brigade marched into the picturesque old city that nestled quaintly on the sides of the fabled and enchanted Cerro de Moctezuma, Moctezuma's Hill, a city that had been born within a generation of the conquest. It had an old-world appearance with its cathedral-fronted square, rough, cobblestone streets, and old-fashioned markets. There were palaces here like that of Don Manuel Tomas de la Canal, the wealthy *Hidalgo* who built the little Chapel of the Casa de Loreto which, because of the poetry of its color and hand carving, some have called frozen music, with dulcet melodies that congealed when it was fashioned.

Here in San Miguel during the War for Independence Father Hidalgo and the patriot Allende had waved the Banner of the Virgin of Guadalupe, and here the Queen's Regiment had suddenly and miraculously joined the weak insurgent forces, which had then grown into a victorious patriot army. And here during the last days of the Empire the bitter tides of battle would ebb and flow, and grim, white-bearded old Carterac would call out to the Third Zouaves as they fixed their bayonets and prepared to charge, "My Children, the Third know how to die. One more victory and one more cross for all of you. Forward!" So he then would smile and lead them forward; but after the smoke should clear they would find that he had gone but a little way in advance of his children.

A gallant, gaily uniformed and caparisoned regiment galloped from the city gates to meet Shelby and his men as they entered San Miguel. The arms of Carlota were embroidered on the blue of the royalist uniforms and above them flew a silken flag said to have been wrought by her gentle hands, a flag unbaptized as yet by blood or battle.

At the head of the regiment rode Colonel Miguel Lopez, the pampered darling of the Imperial Court, with his fair Saxon face and his handsome Norman features, a Centaur in the saddle and a royal courtier, but the same Lopez who, ere many months should pass, would become the traitor of Queretaro, the wretch who dishonored his flag, betrayed his regiment, abandoned his Empress, and sold out his Emperor for thirty thousand dollars in gold. But he would make full payment for his treason, for, as was afterwards written: "Is it any wonder that his wife for-

View of Queretaro, from a contemporary print.

sook him, that his children turned their faces away from him, that the church refused him asylum, that a righteous soldier of the Liberal cause smote him upon either cheek in the presence of an army on parade, and that even the very *lazzaroni* of the streets pointed at him as he passed, and shouted in voluble derision: 'The Traitor! The Traitor!!' " And they still tell in the City of Mexico how he became a wandering outcast, was bitten one day by a mad dog, and died of hydrophobia.

Colonel Lopez and his command escorted the Brigade through the town to a camp site where it bivouacked.

Then on to Queretaro, the old Otomi Indian town, scene of the day-long, prearranged, fist-fight battle between the Otomis and their Spanish and Indian enemies in 1531, which was to become the scene of one of the saddest of Mexican tragedies. For Maximilian would come here during the last days of the Empire; here he would be captured by the Liberals, imprisoned in the old Capuchin convent, tried by a military court on the stage of a theater; and here he would be shot on the gentle

143

slope of the *Cerro de las Campanas,* the Hill of the Bells, a pawn on the chessboard of France's Napoleon the Little.

The Brigade rested in Queretaro and made final preparations for the march to the City of Mexico, now only a scant hundred and thirty miles away.

Edwards described those days with fond remembrance: "Peace stood in the ranks of the sentinel corn, and fed with the cattle that browsed by the streams in the meadows. Peace came on the wings of the twilight and peopled the grasses with songs that soothed, and many toned voices that made for the earth a symphony. Days of short parade and longer merry-making dawned for the happy soldiery . . . Couriers came and went, and told of peace throughout the realm; of robber bands surrendering to the law; of railroads planned and parks adorned; of colonists arriving and foreign ships in all the ports; of roads made safe for travel, and public virtue placed at premium in the market lists; of prophecies that brightened all the future."

The Brigade also re-outfitted at Queretaro, for the entrance into the Imperial Capital must be grandly and brilliantly made. The men worked at their Spanish and practiced little courtly phrases which could be used to advantage in the salons of the palaces and in the cafes and *tivolis.* Drills became more exact and precise in movement and salutes more flamboyantly given. The dust and the heat and the hardship of the weary, long miles faded into the past, and with their fading the pride of the Old Brigade, with its dash and *élan,* returned.

Shelby reveled in this rebirth of spirit and when the day came, rode proudly at the head of his men as they began the pleasant, last march to the City of the Palaces, the Seat of Empire.

VII

THE FALLEN
GUIDON

19. The City of Mexico

THE ROAD from Queretaro to the City of Mexico ran
through a land filled with fields of grain and grazing
stock, and past *haciendas* and *ranchos* which flew the
flag of the Emperor. No guerrillas lurked in the hills or at the
river fords, for French troops patrolled the roads and garrisoned
important towns and villages. It was glorious summer in the high
plateau land of central Mexico and the expedition moved by
easy stages, so it was a holiday for cavalrymen accustomed to
long forays and forced campaigns.

They passed along the eastern edge of Queretaro, under the
old aqueduct which had been built during the last part of the
previous century and along the floor of the valley which sloped
upward to the village of Ahorcada and the rugged mountain
divide, then dropped down the eastern ridges to San Juan del
Rio and on through green valleys nestled among hills that
threatened to become mountains toward the ancient Indian town
of Tula.

One night they camped near the little village of Linares. The
Alcalde, a wealthy *hacendado,* had been to California, spoke a
little English, and loved Americans for but two attributes—
their hard swearing and their hard drinking. The great love of
his life was his fighting cocks—for cock fighting, along with bull
fighting, was the national pastime of Mexico—and he owned
two hundred of them. In a burst of generosity and friendship
he proposed that Shelby and his command wait over a day that
he might give them some pleasure with the birds.

That night the men sat around the camp drinking, smoking
and spinning fantastic tales and ready-made legends of the brave
days that were past and dead. Perhaps some of them were

145

dreaming of more northern climes, of farms and villages in Arkansas and Missouri where they had lived and where lived their families and, for a few of them, wives and children.

John Thrailkill sat by his fire—Thrailkill the old guerrilla of the Missouri-Kansas border, the warrior who never slept, the knight-errant who wore the small black flag fastened to the crown of his hat. Thrailkill was one of the deadliest soldiers of the Old Brigade and one of its best pistol shots. He had served through four years of war and now, as was his want, he was reminiscent—tales of border fighting, stories of camp pranks and jokes, battle sagas when he had fought against desperate odds and by sheer bravado had won. As the night wore on he became garrulous, the odds mounted, and braggadocio crept into his words and tones and gestures. The listeners smiled and urged him on—all except one. Anthony West was frankly doubtful, saw no humor in the telling and presently ridiculed the narrator.

Though not usually swift to anger, Thrailkill rose with quivering lips and bristling beard: "You disbelieve me, it seems, and for the skeptic there is only the logic of a blow." He bent low so he could look into West's eyes. "Is this real, and this?" And he slapped West twice in the face with the back of his hand; a taunting, unpardonable insult. Friends instantly stepped in between them, but the damage had been done, the insult had been given.

The men went to bed, but Captain James Gillette soon came to Thrailkill.

"I have a message for you."

"It is not long, I hope."

"Not very long, but very plain."

"Yes, yes, they are all alike. I have seen such before. Wait for me a few minutes."

Thrailkill arose and in a few minutes routed Ike Berry from his blankets. Berry and Gillette agreed to the terms of the duel—Colt's revolvers, one loaded, the other empty. The two guns were placed under a blanket with only the butts exposed. The men drew lots for the choice and Thrailkill won. He stooped down and pulled out one of the weapons. It was the loaded revolver. Tomorrow at sunset West would be a dead man.

The next day was the *fiesta* of the cocks. Shelby sent the

Alcalde a case of fine cognac, which had been a gift of General Douay, and completely won his heart. Ah, these Southerners—noble, knightly, men of spirit—who thronged the town and mingled freely with the holiday-minded *ciudadanos.*

At noon the cock pit, with its tiers of seats rising in ever-widening full circles, was filled. *Hacendados, rancheros, vaqueros, peon* farmers thronged into the amphitheatre; *señoritas* gave furtive, inviting glances to the soldiers; priests mingled with their parishioners and wagered on their favorite cocks. The *Alcalde* placed Shelby at his right in the Governor's box above the entrance.

The bugle sounded and the birds were weighed and matched. The heels, those curved, razor-sharp, little swords fastened at the back of the leg, were put on. The matches began and throughout the afternoon there was death and life in the pit and the constant changing of pesos by those who still had silver. Thrailkill lost heavily and steadily. The eighteenth fight came up and he had no money to wager. Gillette, West's second in the forthcoming duel, walked over.

"You do not bet and the battle is about to begin."

"I do not bet because I have not won. The pitcher that goes eternally to a well is certain to be broken at last."

"And yet you are fortunate."

Thrailkill shrugged. It was still an hour before sunset.

"You have no money, then. Would you like to borrow?"

"No."

An old priest wandered over to Thrailkill. "A doubloon to a doubloon against the black cock."

This was too much for Thrailkill. He weakened and looked at Gillette.

Gillette spoke quietly and slowly, words filled with tension and emotion, and with meaning: "You do not want to kill West—the terms are murderous—you have been soldiers together—you can take the priest's bet—here is the money. But if you win you pay me—if you lose I have absolute disposal of your fire."

Thrailkill straightened. "Ah! what would you do with my fire?"

"Keep your hands clean from innocent blood, John Thrailkill. Is not that enough?"

Thrailkill took the doubloon, laid his wager. The battle took

147

but a moment and a cock lay dead upon the sand of the small arena. Thrailkill had won. He still controlled his fire.

The cock fights ended and the small group of men withdrew beyond the edge of the village. The secret had been well kept; only those who had sat around the fire and had witnessed the insult were there. Gillette was calm, but there were traces of anticipation and hope in his eyes. Berry's expression was sorrowful; he had not been able to prevent the meeting and he loved both men. West took his position, a tragic but composed figure who had drunk deeply from the cup of life and who now was prepared to taste its last bitter drops with unmoved serenity. No trace of expression crossed the face of John Thrailkill. There he stood—stern, cold, merciless.

Around them floated the peaceful sounds of evening—the lowing cattle being driven in to their corrals, the songs and talk of field workers on their way to low, flat-roofed, mud-brick and plastered huts, the flutter and chirping of birds, the bubbling of the near-by stream. Over toward the west the sun was sinking in all its pristine glory among the rugged peaks of the cordilleras. Then came the ringing tones of the church bells, the Angelus giving the call to vespers.

The preliminaries ended. The command was given. West never moved, never changed expression, as Thrailkill threw up his revolver and leveled it. But no shot came. Thrailkill looked hard at his victim, bored deeply into his eyes but saw no fear there, only calm resignation to the inevitable, to death. With a jerk, he raised the heavy-calibre revolver and fired a single shot into the sky.

The Brigade moved on, passed Marques and Tula, Huehuetoca and Coyotepec, and finally mounted the rim of the Valley of Mexico at its northwestern edge. Reaching the crest, the men looked over the great valley, some forty miles wide and eighty miles long, one of the most spectacular elongated depressions in the entire world, and, nestled near the southern end, bordered on the east and southeast by the lakes, they saw the City of Mexico.

As they moved down the gentle slopes they passed through more towns and villages—Tepozotlan, with its 16th century Seminario de San Martin and church, among the more beautiful ex-

148

View of the City of Mexico, from an old print.

amples of colonial ecclesiastical architecture in all Mexico, Cuautitlan, Tlalnepantla, and Azcapotzalco. At last they came to Tacuba. Here the Brigade bivouacked for the last time.

The next morning the Brigade passed through Popotla, where Cortez the Conqueror wept for his slain men underneath the Ahuehuete tree, *el arbol de la noche triste* (the tree of the sad night), after his army had broken out of Aztec Tenochtitlan. Looking to the right as they passed through the Gate of Santo Tomas, the men saw the cemetery where the Americans who had been killed or who had died in the Valley during Winfield Scott's campaign in the Mexican War were buried. They moved up San Cosme Street, entered Puente de Alvarado Street and crossed the narrow canal over which that conquistador is supposed to have made his noted leap. Turning south, they passed El Caballito, the noted bronze statue to the emperor Charles IV, and galloped down the Paseo de Bucareli to the Ciudadela, the old fortress which had been designated as their headquarters.

149

They debouched on the plaza which fronted the building and went into camp. It was the third of September.

The long march to the fabled City of Mexico had ended—from the rolling hills of east Texas, through Austin and San Antonio and across arid, southern plains, through rugged Mexican cordilleras, over dry tablelands and through the green-filled valleys of central Mexico; over two thousand miles of intermittent battles with unfriendly elements and with even more unfriendly American and Mexican guerrillas.

Shelby's first duty was to provide for the care and comfort of Inez Walker, who had accompanied the expedition since the fight at the *hacienda* of La Encarnacion. Freed from the captivity of her abductor and removed from the terrors of that night of butchery at the *hacienda,* she recovered much of her lost beauty and became a favorite in Mexico City society and a close friend of Princess Agnes Salm-Salm, a Southern girl married to the noted Prussian adventurer who was now in the service of the Emperor. The two were frequently seen at social functions or driving with Her Majesty along the Alameda or the Paseo Bucareli or the newly-opened boulevard now called the Paseo de la Reforma.

John Edwards, with a few companions, had been sent ahead into the City of Mexico and had arrived five or six days before. He had not been idle in his search for information and he now reported to his commander.

During the preceding three months many Southerners had arrived in the capital and some had already found service with the Empire. Commodore Matthew Fontaine Maury had been appointed Imperial Commissioner of Immigration. General John B. Magruder had been named chief of the Colonization Land Office. General B. H. Lyon of Kentucky and General John McCausland of Virginia had become government surveyors; General W. H. Stevens, former chief engineer on Lee's staff, had been made chief engineer of the Mexican Imperial Railway, while Governor Thomas C. Reynolds was now the superintendent of two short-line railroads running out from the City of Mexico, and ex-Governor Henry Watkins Allen of Louisiana was ready to begin publication of the government-sponsored *Mexican Times.* Many new arrivals had established plantations, lumber mills, or other businesses or had secured employment; still other ex-Confederates were sojourning in Mexico until they could find means to continue their journey to Central or South America, the islands of the West Indies, or Europe.

Small groups of Southern expatriates were constantly arriving. On the tenth of August ex-Governor Allen had written to his friend Sarah Dorsey, that "Generals Price and Polk, of Missouri, and Judge Perkins [of Louisiana] arrived today. They are all well. Thank God! we are all, at least, beyond the power of persecution, prisons and chains. Judge Perkins looks in fine health."

Many ex-soldiers awaited the arrival of Shelby and his force, for they had heard that he planned to take service under the Emperor and they hoped to enlist in his army of ex-Southerners.

But, during the march from San Luis Potosi, there had been disheartening rumors that Maximilian did not favor Shelby's scheme to enlist an army of ex-Confederates and recently discharged Federals to serve his Empire. Shelby had disregarded them: "We can get forty thousand and take our pick. Young men for war, and only young men emigrate. . . . It appears to me that we shall soon see the sky again. What do *you* say, Captain?" And he had turned to Langhorne.

"The French are not friendly—that is to say, they want no soldiers from among us. You will not be permitted to recruit even so much as a front and a rear rank; and if this is what you mean by seeing the sky, then the sky is as far away as ever."

Later events bore Langhorne out. General Magruder, who had known Bazaine in the Crimea, had spoken twice with the Marshal and on each occasion had received the same reply, "Bid Shelby march immediately to Mexico." General William B. Preston had begged for permission to go north to meet Shelby with authority for him to enlist a corps, but received the same order, "Bid Shelby to march immediately to Mexico."

Edwards now reported that there were many unfavorable portents. A law had been passed against foreigners—they could hold no property unless they became citizens of Mexico, nor could a man take service with the government unless he became naturalized. William M. Gwin and General Charles P. Stone

151

were having difficulties with their Sonora colonization scheme.

The men of the Brigade were well acquainted with the city within twenty-four hours after their arrival. They visited the centers of the city's night life: the cafes—the Veroly, Magnan's, the Cafe del Progreso, the Noche Buena, and Sylvain's; or the *tivolis*—the open-air gardens which served food and drink; and some of them even gained entrance to the Lonja Club, the most important in the city.

They attended the theatres, perhaps heard Donizetti's "El Belisario" at the Imperial, or went to the Iturbide to laugh at the French comedy, "The Mysteries of Summer," or to the Principal to see Señor del Castrillo in the popular drama *"Pobres y Ricos."* A few probably heard the Sunday morning military masses at the Cathedral. Undoubtedly they all witnessed the celebrations of the 16th of September, Mexico's 4th of July: the early dawn band concert at the *Zocalo* (the great square fronting the Cathedral and the National Palace), the grand military parade, the afternoon free bull fight at the Plaza de Toros del Paseo, and the crowds entering the Imperial Theater for the evening's musical program, "the ladies in their most elegant toilettes" and wearing "such a display of rare and costly jewels" as Henry Watkins Allen had never seen.

Some of them probably patronized the Hotel San Agustin where "choice liquors and ices . . . good billiard tables, baths—cold or warm" were to be had at all times and were dispensed in four languages. Others conceivably attended the grand opening of the "New Saloon" at the Hotel Nacional, where F. Dufere, late of the St. Louis Hotel, New Orleans, was "prepared to satisfy the most fastidious taste in the art of mixing liquors, and preparing elegant drinks." They hired carriages or horses and rode along the paseo or in the parks with the afternoon parade of citizens.

Though the language problem was a difficult one, they soon mastered such necessary phrases as *a los pies de usted, señorita* (at your feet, lady), *con su permiso* (with your permission), and others, and began to use the exaggerated and excessively-given bows and handshakings and the *embrazo,* the traditional embrace used by masculine friends when greeting each other. It was not long before some of them were "playing the bear"

152

Plaza and church of San Domingo in Mexico City.

(walking up and down under their lady's window), speaking with their arms and hands in the sign language of the country (as for example the closed fist struck against the chest which signified extravagant admiration of a woman), indulging in a *pelando la pava* (flirtation) at a barred window, and using such love-making phrases as *hija de mi alma* (little girl of my soul) or *preciosita de mis ojos* (little precious one of my eyes).

It is not altogether improbable that a few of them memorized the Spanish words to the *"Aforrado"* song, which began

Lining of my life!
How are you? How do you do?
How have you passed the night?
Have you met with nothing new?

and which ended

And come then with me,
And I will give thee
Such fine shoes of satin,
The color of tea.

After all, the City of Mexico had a population of nearly a quarter of a million; there was a lot to do.

153

One of them, James Wood, served as the second of Dr. L. C. Hassell of South Carolina in his duel with a Belgian Major of the French Foreign Legion.

One afternoon the Princess Salm-Salm was sitting quietly in a cafe. The Belgian, knowing that she had been an actress and an equestrienne in a circus, boisterously called out a derisive circus slang term and shouted: "Hoop la!" The French officers laughed at the inference of the Belgian, and the Austrians applauded. Dr. Hassell was present and immediately went to his American countrywoman.

"You have been insulted. I knew it, or rather, I may say I saw it. Not understanding German, if, indeed, the Belgians speak German, I have to rely for my opinion more upon the manner than the matter of the insult. Your husband is away, you are an American lady, you are a countrywoman of mine, you are in trouble and you need a protector. Will you trust your honor in my hands?"

She was a soldier's wife and she well knew that a duel would follow. Hassell walked over to the Belgian.

"Do you speak English?"

"A little."

"Enough to understand the truth when I tell it to you?"

"Perhaps, if it is not so plain that for the telling I will have to break every bone in your body." The Belgian spoke loudly. The spectators stopped eating and leaned toward the speakers.

"That lady who has just gone out is a countrywoman of mine. She may have been an actress just as you may have been a hangman's son, but whatever she has been she is a woman. We do not insult women in the country where I once lived, nor do we permit it to be done elsewhere. Will you apologize to her?"

"I will not."

"Will you accept this card and let me send a friend to you?"

"I will with pleasure."

Wood made the arrangements and the two men met the next morning in an open field a short distance south of Shelby's headquarters. Hassell lost the toss and so had to face the sun. Both men missed at the first fire, but on the second Hassell seriously wounded his adversary in the shoulder. The Southerners carried Hassell away for a celebration.

154

20. The Conference With the Emperor

THE DREAMER of Miramar had been emperor of Mexico a little over a year when Shelby and his men arrived. The story of his coming had been a tale of international intrigue and high finance. During the years before 1860 Mexico had gotten heavily into debt with French, English and Spanish nationals and when the debts were not paid these nationals had protested to their governments. The three powers met in London in 1861 and agreed to send a joint expedition to Mexico. Vera Cruz was occupied in 1862, but the United States protested and the Spanish and English troops were speedily withdrawn, leaving France alone and unsupported.

In May, 1863, General Elie Frederic Forey occupied Puebla with a force of twelve thousand men; President Benito Juarez and the Liberal army evacuated the capital; and in June the French troops marched triumphantly into the old City of the Palaces. France and the Conservative-Clerical party began to work together toward the founding of a Mexican monarchy.

An Assembly of Notables convened in July and a few days later submitted a plan which provided for an hereditary, limited monarchy, with the title "Emperor of Mexico," and offered the crown to Prince Ferdinand Maximilian, Archduke of Austria. Maximilian accepted, was crowned Emperor of Mexico, reached Vera Cruz in late May, 1864, and proceeded at once to his new capital.

He was received by the aristocracy, the wealthy and the Church dignitaries with royal and ritualistic pomp and circumstance, but the Liberals under Juarez ignored him, despite his appeals for their cooperation, and the citizens of the capital began singing or repeating a grim jingle:

So you're here, Maximilian!
And now that you came,
What's left of what have you, my brother,
Is going to remain.

After a sort of second coronation, Archbishop Pelagio Labastida organized a great demonstration and from the balcony of his palace made an impassioned speech to the throng, closing with "For a thousand and thousands of years, *Viva! Viva!*"

155

It had been an effective show. The rank and file of the ordinary citizens of the country, with one eye cocked on the French army garrisons, and the other on future imperialistic parades and demonstrations, with their hands putting ready cash in their pockets because of temporary prosperity, and realizing that they were powerless anyway, settled down to await developments. Within a week Maximilian had organized his cabinet. The Mexican Empire was an accomplished fact.

Few would have argued the point. The French army occupied every important city in Mexico, from Vera Cruz to Guadalajara, from Morelia to San Luis Potosi, from Cuernavaca to Monterrey. But "Don Benito" held on, he and his ill-organized, ill-fed, ill-equipped armies. Juarez was "not a three-minute trotter, but a mighty good all-day horse, and safe for a long journey," as one of his friends, a horse fancier, had said. All Maximilian and the French could do was to hold the important towns, all they "ever owned, or occupied, or controlled, or felt safe in, was that extent of territory and no more which their cannon covered."

Only the United States had raised a voice of protest against the conquest of Mexico and that government was now fighting for its life in a civil war. But the United States left no doubt as to its position. Three weeks before Maximilian landed at Vera Cruz, tall but stout, awkward-gaited, double-chinned Thomas Corwin, the American Minister, left the City of Mexico, ostensibly on leave of absence. The day would come when the American Civil War would end; meanwhile, Abraham Lincoln urged Benito Juarez to hold on.

The war had now ended. President Andrew Johnson and Secretary of State William H. Seward were putting pressure on Napoleon III to withdraw his troops and General William Tecumseh Sherman was marching with a strong army toward the Rio Grande.

Marshal Bazaine knew that the days of the French in Mexico were numbered. The ex-Confederates who were thronging into the country knew the Emperor would need help. Maximilian should have known it. Shelby had arrived with several hundred men, and he was in a position to enlist a much larger force for the service of the Emperor. For Maximilian the hour and the man who might have saved him had met.

156

Upon his arrival in the City of Mexico, Shelby went directly to the Hotel San Carlos, at what is today the corner of Madero and Bolivar streets, the headquarters of the ex-Confederate exiles. Magruder and Maury had already conferred with the Emperor's confidential secretary and had arranged an audience for Shelby.

Shelby and his aide, Major John Edwards, accompanied by General John B. Magruder and Commodore Matthew Fontaine Maury, were received by the Emperor in one of the informal reception rooms of the Palacio Nacional, the old two-storied colonial building fronting the great square. With the Emperor were Marshal Bazaine and Count de Noue, the Chief of Bazaine's civil staff, who would serve as interpreter.

Maximilian welcomed Shelby without ceremony and with apparent frankness and sincerity. Shelby was impressed with the man who had come from his fanciful palace of Miramar on the shores of the Adriatic to become the Emperor of the Mexicans. He was in his early thirties, over six feet in height, slender, with a high forehead and clear, blond complexion, flaxen hair and a full yellow beard which fell in a wave on his chest. He had the Hapsburg mouth and lower lip, "that thick, protruding, semi-cleft under lip, too heavy for beauty, too immobile for features that, under the iron destiny that ruled the hour, should have suggested Caesar or Napoleon." He had blue eyes and his expression was serene and complacent, even gentle. He looked the part of an athlete, and it was well known that he was a splendid horseman and that few men could hold their own with him with broadsword or rapier.

But Shelby had already been informed that he was a poetic, lethargic dreamer, that he was no soldier and had no mind for politics, that he was indecisive and frequently forgot promises. Perhaps Shelby saw the weakling in him, the temperamental, vacillating weakling who in the days to come would be beaten in his last well-meant efforts to secure the public good and who would permit his advisers and officials to turn him into a tyrant, staking the crown of Mexico on desperate resolves and cruel, even savage, actions. Such figures were not new to the world's great stage, but they had never founded empires.

What chance would such a man have against Benito Juarez,

157

the low, squat Indian whom the aristocrats and *hacendados* and Church dignitaries laughed at, with his strong, purposeful face "scarred with the small pox like Mirabeau's," with his tenacious will and idealism, and "his sleuth-hound ways that followed the trail of the Republic, though in the scent there was pestilence and famine and death"; Benito Juarez, who led forty thousand scattered and ragged men, speaking all dialects, against the magnificently-equipped and well-trained legions of the French, unappeasable and murderous; Juarez, the great Liberal, who would yet live to drive out the Austrian and recreate the Mexican Republic.

In Bazaine, Shelby saw a far different man than the Emperor. He was about fifty years of age, had a strong, positive face, crowned by white hair, where there was hair, and completely bald over the front portion, as was true with most Frenchmen who had served long years in northern Africa. His long, lithe, fit body was set on short legs. He was an aristocrat, married to a wealthy Mexican girl, brutal in discipline but somewhat beloved of his troops and his military family for his bravery, frankness and soldierly qualities. He was a skilled and crafty soldier, was well as an able administrator. On the debit side, however, Shelby had heard that he was a gambler and a speculator who was making a fortune in Mexico through the importation of duty-free goods.

There was too much contrast between the two men. Maximilian had not seriously wanted the crown in the first place; he had preferred his brilliant little mimic court at Miramar where he could write verse and compose songs; it had been Carlota who had wanted the sceptre. He was a pawn on the chessboard of politics, moved here and there by Napoleon the Little, and a puppet to Bazaine, who was the real ruler of Mexico.

But Shelby's Rubicon had been crossed a thousand miles northward at the Rio Grande; he had planned for this moment since his men had voted for the Empire against the Republic of the Indian. He confidently proceeded to lay his plans before the Emperor.

He would take immediate service in the forces of Maximilian and recruit an army of forty thousand men from ex-Confederates

158

who were thronging to Mexico and from Northerners who were being mustered out of the United States Army. This army would stand as a bulwark against the day when the French forces would be withdrawn from Mexico.

"It is only a question of time, Your Majesty, before the French soldiers are withdrawn."

"Why do you think so?" asked the Emperor.

"Because the War Between the States is at an end, and Mr. Seward will insist on the rigorous enforcement of the Monroe Doctrine. France does not desire a conflict with the United States. It would neither be popular nor profitable."

The Emperor listened.

"I left behind me a million men in arms, not one of whom has yet been discharged from the service. The nation is sore over this occupation, and the presence of the French is a perpetual menace."

He paused, then continued: "I hope Your Majesty will pardon me, but in order to speak the truth it is necessary to speak plainly."

"Go on," ordered Maximilian.

Shelby argued that his plan was perfectly feasible and practicable, that he had good authority for believing that the American government would not oppose the enlistment of ex-Confederates or disbanded Union troops in the service of the Empire, and that the United States would not oppose the Empire if it could be demonstrated that it could stand without the power of a French army.

"In order to put yourself in a position to do this," Shelby continued, "and in order to sustain yourself sufficiently long to consolidate your occupation of Mexico and make your Government a strong one, I think it absolutely necessary that you should have a corps of foreign soldiers devoted to you personally, and reliable in any emergency."

The Emperor asked for the opinions of Magruder and Maury, who agreed with Shelby and added arguments of their own.

Shelby continued that he would encourage immigration to Mexico in every possible way, that he would develop the resources of the country and would hold it with a strong and well-disciplined army until such time as the people became recon-

159

ciled to the Empire and convinced of its stability and could see evidences of economic progress.

"I have under my command at present about 1,000 tried and experienced troops. All of them have seen much severe and actual service, and all of them are anxious to enlist in support of the Empire."

Bazaine had listened closely to Shelby's arguments and his judgment was strongly in favor of them, for he knew the time was not far off when he and his troops would be ordered out of Mexico. The tension showed in his face, for it flushed and he nervously toyed with the papers in his hand.

Perhaps he saw in his mind that day almost two years hence when Austrian and Belgian volunteers would be preparing to make the last desperate, futile, charge for the Empire, when Young Lieutenant Karnak would say, "This last charge will soon be over, boys, and there won't be many of us killed, because there are so few of us to kill; but (and he whispered it while the bugles were blowing) although we die for our Emperor to-day, he will die for us to-morrow."

Finally Maximilian arose and beckoned to De Noue. He moved to one side, talked with him for a few minutes, then walked from the room. The prince of the Hapsburgs, the brother of the Emperor Francis Joseph, had refused practical arguments in the complete, though misguided, confidence of his own destiny. Have patience, it was only a question of time until he would be accepted by all Mexicans.

De Noue spoke to Shelby. "It's no use," he said. The Emperor would try to negotiate with the United States. If he could demonstrate to the Americans that he desired to bring good government to Mexico, to develop the country and to educate the people, that government would surely recognize him and enter into friendly relations with his Empire.

"It is no use I say again, General, the Emperor will not give you employment."

"I knew it," replied Shelby.

"How?"

"From his countenance. Not once could I bring the blood to his calm benignant face. He has faith, but no enthusiasm, and enthusiasm such as he needs would be but another name for audacity. I say to you in all frankness, Count De Noue, Maximilian will fail in his diplomacy."

"Your reason, General."

"Because he will not have time to work the problem out."

Shelby explained that he had marched with his men from Piedras Negras, through Monterrey and Saltillo and San Luis Potosi and Queretaro, to the City of Mexico, that he had observed the tenor of the people.

"Save the ground held by your cantonments and your garrisons," he said, "and the ground your cannon can hold in range, and your cavalry can patrol and scour, you have not one foot in sympathy with you, with the Emperor, with the Empire . . . Juarez lives as surely in the hearts of the people as the snow is eternal on the brow of Popocatepetl, and ere an answer could come from Seward to the Emperor's Minister of State, the Emperor will have no Minister of State."

Shelby had finished. Why explain to Bazaine and De Noue that which they should already know.

He turned again to De Noue, "I thank you very much for your kind offices to-day, and would have given a good account of my Americans if king-craft had seen the wisdom of their employment. I must go back to my men now. They expect me early."

Shelby walked down the stone stairs and through the broad entrance hallway into the sunlight of the Great Plaza.

The Emperor was a dreaming fool. He thought of Mexico as another Italian province, another Lombardo-Venitian kingdom, where he had governed without disturbances and had fatuously believed that he had been beloved by the people. He never stopped to think that he had had an army at his back, a strong Austrian army, and that Field Marshal Joseph Radetzky had plundered and slain until the Italians were completely without resources for continued resistance and without spirit for a hopeless cause.

The expedition of Shelby and his men had been doomed from the beginning, for Bazaine had mistrusted their motives and had been misinformed of their numbers and movements since entering Mexico. The Emperor's mind had been completely led astray from real issues and problems and poisoned by his

161

Conservative and Church counselors. In addition, he was far too busy with his butterflies and his poetry to hear the dim murmurings of the people and the rumblings of the gathering storm in the north, or to attempt to understand the deep and indomitable character of Juarez, who was soon to rush southward from Coahuila and Chihuahua with his ragged hordes to uproot a doomed dynasty with fire and blood. Let them laugh at the Indian.

But the Empire held out for nearly two years, while Maximilian grew steadily more indecisive and the country burst into flames.

Maximilian continued his banquets and dinners and small, intimate *tertulias*—during the first six months of 1865 he had given thirty-six such functions at which he entertained over thirty-five hundred guests. He continued his coarse after dinner tales and jests and openly admired certain ladies of the court who, in his own words, "ought to be formidable women to love." Young José Luis Blasio, his valet, reported that his bedroom in the Palacio Nacional, easily accessible because of secret doors, "was visited many times by ladies of the court, who slipped in and out so mysteriously that only I saw them, and frequently without knowing who they were." After Carlota returned to Europe in July, 1866, to beg for assistance for his dying Empire he had a more open affair with a girl at Cuernavaca, concerning which one of the French officers wrote to Paris: "The Emperor and the empire remain as unpopular here as ever. Everyone awaits their collapse. But Maximilian's great occupation is his continual trips to Cuernavaca to visit the young Mexican by whom he is to have a child; proud in this proof of his capacity for parenthood. Meanwhile the country is without direction, without confidence, and without a *soul!*"

A week after Carlota's departure the United States Congress officially recognized the Juarez government, and Colonel Vicente Riva Palacio published in *El Pito Real* his noted song *Adios Mama Carlota,* which became the marching song of the Republicans. Bazaine gradually withdrew his forces from the distant towns during the fall of 1866 and Juarez immediately occupied them. The noose was tightening around the neck of the Austrian.

The United States increased its pressure upon Napoleon the

Little and by the end of the year only a few cities were held by the French and the Emperor. Bazaine urged abdication, but during a retreat at Jalapilla the Emperor vacillated between remaining in the country or abdicating. General Eduard de Castelnau arrived from France to urge relinquishing the crown, but Maximilian refused to see him—he had at last "committed himself to remaining on the throne."

The American frigate *Susquehanna* appeared off the harbor at Vera Cruz bearing General William T. Sherman, on a voyage of reconnaissance, and Lewis Campbell, who would become the new Minister to Mexico when Benito Juarez returned to the Capital.

The Junta of Notables met in middle January, 1867. General Leonardo Marquez was positive that the Imperialists would triumph; Tomas Murphy considered the Juarez forces no more than "bands of thieves"; while Alejandro Arango y Escandon drew parallels from European history and prophesied that "the imperial throne of Mexico" would soon shine with the brilliance of a pacified country. On the twenty-first Maximilian returned to the City of Mexico and was greeted by an indifferent citizenry.

But the opera company, hearing rumors of the imminent departure of the French troops and anticipating the fall of the Empire, set out for Vera Cruz. Foreign owned business houses began to wind up their affairs, while French civilians made preparations to leave the country. Then on the morning of February fifth the last of the French troops started for home, while Prince Felix zu Salm-Salm stood on the balcony of the Iturbide Palace on Madero Street and through his monocle contemptuously gazed at the final humiliation of Napoleon III. Behind one of the parapets of the Palacio Nacional "a tall man, wrapped in a gray cloak with a wide felt hat on his head, followed with his eyes the ranks of the French rear guard, and when they had disappeared turned to the group of gentlemen surrounding him and said: 'At last we are free!' " Poor, foolish Max; within a few weeks he would be hopelessly besieged at Queretaro.

The dark hour was upon Saul. The attitude of the Church changed; the treasury was empty; corruption and falsehood were

163

on every hand; men on whom he and the Empress had lavished favors were fleeing the approaching cataclysm. Only a handful remained—Tomas Mejia the Indian, Miguel Miramon, Ramon Mendez, Leonardo Marquez, and a few others—and with the coming of the final days some of these would desert him.

But Max had been through his Gethsemane. At this time a new man emerges and his incapacity as a leader is forgotten, his intellectual limitations are overlooked. History forgot his weaknesses and his shortcomings when she saw how well he could die.

He occupied Queretaro and Juarez's lines began to tighten. Lieutenant Karnak gathered his seventy men around him and rushed headlong against the enemy, and only a half dozen came back—without their gallant leader. Young Ramon Mendez, the "lion in combat," weak from illness and shot through the arm, was strapped to the saddle—"I want to die in the harness"; another shot carried away part of his chin, another lodged in his right shoulder, a fourth killed his horse, which fell and pinned him underneath, and, lying thus, a fusillade of shots finished him. But betrayers of the Empire were also at work.

At last the Emperor rode out with a white flag and surrendered to a Colonel Green, who commanded the American Legion from San Francisco. Green took him to General Mariano Escobedo. The Emperor drew his sword and said, "I am Maximilian, Emperor of Mexico. I am the Emperor no longer, but a Mexican citizen, and your prisoner." But Escobedo coldly looked him over and replied: "No, Maximilian, you are not now Emperor, and never were!" The deed was done; the second Mexican Empire belonged to History.

They tried him, almost as a common criminal, while appeals poured in on Juarez to spare the life of the damned. The military tribunal convicted him and Princess Salm-Salm threw herself at Juarez's feet to plead for his life, but the implacable Indian only said: "If all the kings and queens of Europe were in your place I could not spare that life. It is not I who take it, it is the people and the law."

The Emperor heard the false news of Carlota's death (she would live on in her insanity until 1927)—"One tie less to bind me to the world." He gave his wedding ring to Dr. Samuel

164

Basch, saying simply, "You will tell my mother that I did my duty as a soldier and died like a Christian." Then came the last morning and he looked over the broad, fertile valley of Queretaro with its fields of uncut corn and grazing cattle and said to Father Soria, "What a beautiful view! And what a beautiful day to die!"

They carried him to the Hill of the Bells, *El Cerro de las Campanas,* where he would face the firing squad. He asked the soldiers to shoot straight, for he hated the sight of blood and had placed eight handkerchiefs across his breast underneath the uniform to keep from staining it, and began his rambling incoherent speech to Escobedo, but the foolish words were stopped.

The volley killed Miramon and Mejia instantly, but the men had dreaded firing at the Emperor and so they haggled him; Colonel Sobieski gave his revolver to Sergeant Blanquet, who placed the muzzle behind one ear and pulled the trigger.

The old City of Mexico, under whose trees the soldiers of Cortez had made love in the moonlight their blades not yet dry with the blood of the slain, whose Hill of the Grasshopper had reflected the cold glitter of American steel, whose great square had witnessed scenes of pageantry and degradation, had seen the last of the Austrian. The European Archduke had been no match for the blackcoated, implacable Indian.

Perhaps Jo Shelby envisioned some of these things which were to come as he rode slowly back to his command, past the great Cathedral, through the Plaza de Santo Domingo, and past the Plazuela de la Expiacion (the little plaza of the expiation), whose walls were pitted with the bulletmarks of an emperor's firing squads.

21. The Last Review

As SHELBY rode past the Alameda and the site of the ancient *quemadero,* where high Church dignitaries and Inquisitors had watched their wretched victims writhe behind the flames, and turned southward toward the Brigade's quarters, he was thinking of the men who had followed him from eastern Texas to the heart of Mexico to lay their shields and lances at the feet of the Emperor and his Queen, and how he would have to tell them

165

that the Emperor had refused their offer of fealty and service. It was an unpleasant, but necessary duty. The Brigade's last day was at hand.

As he contemplated the dissolution of his gallant command, perhaps his mind wandered back through the years. His troopers had been the finest cavalry of the War—keen and enduring, desperate in battle, insatiate in their appetite for the excitement of conflict and readily hardened and tempered into reckless, butchering centaurs who made conscience subsidiary to slaughter, and were willing to accept the misfortunes of war with the fatalism of an oriental. They had believed in the ʼurvival of the fittest and had partaken of both victory and defeat. But Glory was the mistress whom they served.

The pre-dawn marches into battle, the roar of cannon and the pall of smoke lying heavy and close to the ground, ahead of them Death—yes, Death is yonder in that battery's haze, in the lines of half-obscured infantry, behind the long rows of earthworks; there Death crouches, half asleep, as some gorged wild beast in its lair. But his men had ridden on. He heard again the neighing of horses, the clanking of steel scabbards, the low voices and the oaths, and the steady tramp, tramp as of waves breaking over low and sandy beaches, and then the steady, ominous roll of battle as of thunder in forested mountains or storm-thrown breakers pounding against cliffs that dropped sheer and clean down to the sea.

Thus Shelby rode back to camp to tell his men of a proffer that had been refused, of a boon that had not been granted, of dreams—new homes to which Southerners could repair, a new country which could be built, a new flag which would take the place of the banner which had been sunk in the waters of the Rio Grande—which would never become reality.

He called the men together and told them of the Emperor's resolution. He had offered their services and had done his best to convince the Austrian of his desperate need of them; Magruder and Maury had added arguments that were stamped with truth. But the Dreamer had been blind. His men were fatalists, as soldiers must be, and they heard him through without emotion.

"We are not wanted," he said, "and perhaps it is best so. Those who have fought as you have for a principle have nothing

166

Imperial palace, City of Mexico, from old print.

more to gain in a war for occupation or conquest. Our necessities are grievous, it is true, and there is no work for us in the line of our profession; but to-day, as upon the first day I took command of you, I stand ready to abide your decision in the matter of our destiny."

The men had expected that.

"If you say we shall march to the headquarters of Juarez, then we shall march, although all of you will bear me witness that at Piedras Negras I counseled immediate and earnest service in his government. You refused then as you will refuse to-day. Why? Because you are all Imperialists at heart just as I am, and because, poor simpletons, you imagined that France and the United States might come to blows at last. Bah! the day for that has gone by. Louis Napoleon slept too long."

Irony swept through him.

"How many of you know enough Spanish to get you a Spanish wife with an acre of bread fruit, twenty-five tobacco plants and a handful of corn? We can not starve, boys."

The tension broke and they laughed, then discussed plans for

167

the future. The Brigade would break up, that was certain. The day of its need had past. The iron discipline that had sustained it through the fierce winds of battle could now be relaxed. Let them rest a while and discuss the future. Let each man plan his own destiny.

Shelby sought the advice of Bazaine. It is believed that he conferred with him at the home of the Stevenson family, who lived in Tacubaya, one of the suburbs. They talked of many things over their wine, and as all soldiers they talked of wars and battles won or lost. In later years, Shelby recalled one part of their conversation.

"I should like more than you may imagine," said the Marshal, "to meet this Grant of yours on the battlefield. He should pick fifty thousand Americans and I fifty thousand Frenchmen."

Shelby answered him frankly, and with a smile. "In that event, Marshal, I fear much that you would be worsted."

Bazaine was a magnanimous and generous man. He ordered his finance officer to pay each man of the Brigade, officers and men alike, the sum of fifty dollars—a two thousand mile march, with skirmishes and pitched battles, with dead and wounded comrades, for fifty dollars. But it was a welcome gift, from a soldier who recognized soldiers when he saw them.

Fifty dollars! They were men again, not beggars. They could plan for the future with this legacy that had fallen as rain on a sun-parched field.

So the men talked and planned, accepting their misfortune as they had accepted the defeat of the South, at peace with themselves in a land where there was no peace, and saddened only by the thought that separation from their comrades was near.

Shelby told them of the Carlota Colony which was being established in the tropical lands below Orizaba in the state of Vera Cruz. Here there were farms and plantations to be hewn from the wilderness as their fathers and grandfathers had hewn the lands of Missouri and Arkansas. California was a new country where fortunes could be made. There were other places—distant, obscure, nebulous.

In the end some of them were to join the Carlota Colony. Others would remain in Mexico to engage in trading or other

168

commercial activities. A few would go to California, to Hawaii, to China and Japan. One small group would march northward and join the forces of Juarez in Sonora. A half-dozen would become treasure hunters, for they heard a tale of pirate treasure buried on a tiny island in the Pacific.

About fifty of them would join the Third Zouaves. They wanted to remain together but the grenadiers and cuirassiers and hussars had to be at least six feet tall and this requirement excluded the shorter men. Then, too, the bearded, picturesquely-uniformed, medaled Zouaves, bronzed by African and Mexican sun, did not take off the turban when speaking to an officer; they saluted, yes, with the palm toward the front, but they never uncovered.

Edwards would edit Henry Watkins Allen's English language newspaper *The Mexican Times* after the latter's death, while Shelby would go into the adventuresome but small profit showing freighting business. After the fall of the Empire both men would return to Missouri to build new careers.

But the majority of them would remain awhile in the Capital and then retrace their steps to homes in the villages, fertile valleys, and wooded mountains of Arkansas and Missouri. And one of this group, a bearded young colonel, would walk into his home after an absence of nearly four years, throw down his hat in mock disgust and joyously complain to his surprised wife: "Good Lord, Sally. Dinner not ready yet?"

The last dress parade. The last review.

The Southern exiles in the city came to the large, open plaza that lay to the north of the Ciudadela. So, too, came French officers and troops of the line, and civil officials of the Empire with their retinues, and citizens of the town.

Martin Kritzer's bugle rang out its blast and the men snapped to attention beside their mounts.

Shelby walked slowly down the line, shaking hands with the men, patting them on the shoulder, calling them by their first names or nicknames acquired during four years of comradeship, recalling half-forgotten incidents—the smuggled whisky keg, the pet bear, the stolen pig, a thousand memories rolling back across the years—straightening a collar or buttoning a button with hands that trembled.

169

Tears, unnoticed perhaps, but unashamed, ran down the bronzed faces of men who had just emerged from a desperately-fought and bloody war, men who had dropped an enemy from his horse with a single, well-placed shot or who had felled him with one sweeping sabre stroke.

The bugle call again sounded and Shelby mounted.

The order ran down the line, "Prepare to mount." And the men stood to horse.

"Mount," and the men swung up, their legs snapping across the cantles of their saddles.

They trooped the colors, with only the old guidon, for they had no flag.

Shelby took his position and the Brigade passed in review as was the custom then, first at the walk, then at the canter, and finally at the gallop, a gallop which became a wild battle charge with the Rebel yell echoing from the time-softened old buildings which had witnessed the paradings of the Conquistadores.

The review ended. The faded, tattered guidon which they had followed was lowered for the last time.

What became of the guidon? No one knows. Perhaps even today it reposes with its memories within the bosom of some Missouri or Arkansas family. Perhaps it was lost. Perhaps it was, as one legend has it, cut into little sections so that each man might keep and treasure a little piece of it. If so, the pieces would have been very small.

For each man the future was unknown. The Empire? Juarez and his shabby, steadfast Liberals? The Carlota Colony? The fabled lands of the Orient or the islands of the western seas? Elusive pirate treasures? Brazil or other countries to the south? These Circes would offer but temporary repose for the body until the mind and soul recovered from the bitterness of defeat.

Their guidon had fallen, yes, but beckoning to each of them from beyond the Rio Grande was the old banner of the Republic with its thirteen stripes and its blue field filled with stars.

METHODS,
MATERIALS,
ACKNOWLEDGMENTS

I FIRST HEARD THIS story as one of a grandfather's tales of the War for Southern Independence, for during that conflict Captain William A. Greever, a young Arkansas cavalryman, had ridden with "Old Jo" on a number of raids and forays, including General Sterling Price's invasion of Missouri in 1864. My grandfather greatly admired the leader of the Iron Brigade and I have little doubt but that he exaggerated in detailing many of Shelby's exploits.

During the years which followed I occasionally ran into Shelby and his expedition to Mexico in my general historical reading and research. Then I told the story to a friend and he began to urge me to write an account of the Brigade's march across Texas and Mexico to the capital of that country. Finally, during a year spent in the City of Mexico in 1943-44, I met several persons whose parents had witnessed Shelby's arrival and the last formation of the outfit. My interest was at last sufficiently aroused and I began to browse for information in the Biblioteca Nacional and the Archivo Nacional de la Nacion.

The research continued after my return to the States. It has been a long and sometimes wearisome task for many of the lesser important details were extremely fugitive and required a great deal of hit-and-miss searching before they were finally pinned down. I made several return trips to Mexico, retraced practically all of Shelby's route of march and visited most of the sites of individual incidents.

The story has been made as accurate as possible and nothing has been added to historical fact. All conversation, excepting that of the opening scene, has been taken from the reminiscent writings of Shelby's adjutant, Major John N. Edwards.

The most important source collection is in the possession of

171

Mrs. Ben Manning, Amarillo, Texas, and consists of scrap books, manuscripts and other materials relating to Shelby and the expedition. Other manuscript sources were found in the Department of Archives, Louisiana State University; the University of Texas Library; the Division of Manuscripts, The Library of Congress; the Missouri Historical Society, St. Louis; the Western Historical Manuscripts Collection, University of Missouri; and the Archivo Nacional de la Nacion, City of Mexico.

The Mexican Times (edited successively by Henry Watkins Allen, John N. Edwards, and C. B. Barksdale), a complete file of which is in the Louisiana State University Library, the New York *Herald,* the New York *World,* the Kansas City *Times,* the Kansas City *Star,* the New Orleans *Picayune,* and various Texas newspapers have yielded considerable minutiae.

The only complete published account of the expedition was written by Major John N. Edwards and is entitled *Shelby's Expedition to Mexico, An Unwritten Leaf of the War,* first published in 1872 and reprinted by his wife in 1889. Other works which have been of assistance include: John N. Edwards, *Shelby and His Men, or the War in the West* (Cincinnati, 1867); Jennie Edwards, comp., *John N. Edwards; Biography, Memoirs, Reminiscences and Recollections* (Kansas City, 1889); and Daniel O'Flaherty, *General Jo Shelby, Undefeated Rebel* (Chapel Hill, 1954), the only biography of the Confederate leader.

The War of the Rebellion: A Compilation of the Official Records of the Union and Confederate Armies, 127 books and index (Washington, 1880-1901), yielded considerable information on events during the late months of the war.

General works on Mexico which were used for factual or background materials include: Hubert Howe Bancroft, *History of Mexico,* 6 vols. (San Francisco, 1883-1888); Hubert Howe Bancroft, *History of the North Mexican States and Texas,* 2 vols. (San Francisco, 1886-1889); Miguel Galindo y Galindo, *La gran Decada Nacional* (Mexico, 1904); Vicente Riva Palacio, and others, *Mexico a Traves de los Siglos,* 5 vols. (Mexico, 1887-1889); Vito Robles, *Saltillo en la Historia y en la Leyenda* (Mexico, 1934); Santiago Roel, *Nuevo Leon, Apuntes Historicos,* 2 vols. (Monterrey, 1938); Jesus Romero Flores, *Mexico, Historia de una Gran Ciudad* (Mexico, 1953).

172

Of all the works on the Maximilian period, S. Basch, *Maximilien au Mexique* (Paris, 1869); Jose Luis Blasio, *Maximiliano intimo, el emperador Maximiliano y su corte; memorias de un secretario particular* (Mexico, 1905); Count Egon Caesar Corti, *Maximilian and Charlotte of Mexico* (New York, 1928); M. Payno, *Cuentas, Gastos, Acreedores y otros Asuntos del Tiempo de la Intervencion Francesa y del Imperio* (Mexico, 1868); and Ralph Roeder, *Juarez and His Mexico,* 2 vols. (New York, 1947), have been the most helpful.

Several reminiscences and recollections have yielded numerous details: George Creel, *A Rebel at Large* (New York, 1947); Maurice D'Irisson, Comte d'Herisson, *The Diary of an Interpreter in China* (Annual Report, 1900, Smithsonian Institute, Washington, 1901); Sarah A. Dorsey, *Recollections of Henry Watkins Allen* (New Orleans, 1866); Henry C. McDougal, *Recollections, 1844-1909* (Kansas City, 1910); Sara Yorke Stevenson, *Maximilian in Mexico; A Woman's Reminiscences of the French Intervention, 1862-1867* (New York, 1899); Alexander W. Terrell, *From Texas to Mexico to the Court of Maximilian in 1865* (Dallas, 1933).

William E. Connelley, *Quantrill and the Border Wars* (Cedar Rapids, 1910); Wildred R. Hollister and Harry Norman, *Five Famous Missourians* (Kansas City, 1900); and W. L. Webb, *Battles and Biographies of Missourians* (Kansas City, 1900), were rich in Missouri background material and the last two furnished information on Shelby.

For research or other assistance I especially wish to thank Mrs. Ben Manning of Amarillo, Texas, a descendent of Shelby; my aunt, the late Mrs. John H. Roy, of Harrison, Arkansas, and Spearman, Texas; Mrs. Virginia Ott, of the Department of Archives, Louisiana State University; Mrs. Frances Biese, of the Missouri Historical Society, St. Louis; the late Andres Horcasitas, of the Mexican Tourist Bureau, New Orleans; A. A. Delgado, F. C. Lona, Manuel Santa Maria, and the late Dr. Enrique del Bosque, all of the City of Mexico; Oscar Garza Lozano, of Monterrey, Mexico; Nattie Lee Benson, Librarian of the Latin American Collection, University of Texas; Thomas S. Shaw, Head, Public Reference Section, Library of Congress; Bruce Manning,

Northridge, California; Leon Ogilvie, Kansas City, Missouri; and Barbara Conner for drawing the maps.

For general criticism of the text, I wish to thank R. C. Kemp, Lucille Dutton, Frank Vandiver, John C. L. Andreassen and Donald Ellegood. For practical and detailed assistance during the writing and editing processes, I am deeply indebted to John Loos of the Department of History, Louisiana State University, Edwin A. Davis, Jr., my daughter-in-law, Mary Claire Davis, and my wife, La Verna Rowe Davis, each of whom was an outspoken and uninhibited critic.